Robert Frost

a reference guide

1974-1990

A
Reference
Guide
to
Literature

Robert Frost

a reference guide

1974-1990

PETER VAN EGMOND

G.K.HALL &CO.
70 LINCOLN STREET, BOSTON, MASS.

First published 1991
by G.K. Hall & Co.
70 Lincoln Street
Boston, Massachusetts 02111

10 9 8 7 6 5 4 3 2 1

Library of Congress Cataloging-in-Publication Data

Van Egmond, Peter
Robert Frost: a reference guide, 1974-1990 / Peter Van Egmond.
p. cm. – (Reference guides to literature)
Includes index.
ISBN 0-8161-7271-4
1. Frost, Robert, 1874-1963 – Bibliography. I. Title. II. Series:
Reference guide to literature.
Z8317.78.V36 1991
[PS3511.R94]
016.811'52 – dc20

91-13645
CIP

The paper used in this publication meets the minimum requirements of American National Standard for Information Sciences – Permanence of Paper for Printed Library Materials. ANSI Z39.48-1984. ∞™
MANUFACTURED IN THE UNITED STATES OF AMERICA

Contents

The Author

Peter Van Egmond teaches American literature, specializing in poetry, at the University of Maryland, College Park. He has published and lectured widely on Robert Frost, as well as Walt Whitman, and has recently published the first anthology of American poets for readers in the People's Republic of China. He has been a guest professor at universities in Austria and in China. He is currently working on a critical study of Robert Frost.

Preface

In 1974, G.K. Hall published my *The Critical Reception of Robert Frost*, which was the first attempt to gather critical scholarship on Frost into one volume. That work was not exhaustive, but representative of the main streams of Frost studies. Accordingly, it has been necessary to return to libraries and published works to glean worthwhile material that previously had escaped discovery. The Addendum to the present bibliography begins with 1970, and all the items listed now are those not included in the original book. There are no repetitions of material in that volume.

Assistance in providing citations from Japan was volunteered by Professor Yasuhiro Yoshizaki of Kitakyushu University, Kitakyushu.

Above all, my thanks go to Joan, for making things possible.

Symbols and Abbreviations

*: not verified

passim: throughout the work

DAI: *Dissertations Abstracts International*

o.s.: old series

n.s.: new series

n.p.: no page numbers

AAC: In-house code of UMI Publications indicating dissertation not abstracted

Introduction

When Robert Frost was born in March 1874, this country was approaching only its first centennial. Walt Whitman was still reworking *Leaves of Grass* and would write many more poems. In Britain, Tennyson was yet to be elevated to the peerage. Both those poets would die in 1892, the same year that Frost graduated from high school in Lawrence, Massachusetts, and then entered Dartmouth College for a short time before becoming discouraged – not so much with Dartmouth but with the absence of true direction for his life. He was aware of his fiercely independent nature and of his love for the girl he would insist marry him. He was pretty sure, too, that he would like to be a poet. To that end he had printed up a little book of his poems, which he called *Twilight*, a limited edition certainly, for there were just two copies: one for him and one for Elinor.

The desire to commit himself to love and marriage, and to poetry, must have gnawed at him then and in the years that followed as he tried his hand at a variety of profitless vocations. He was living in a land of great poets and thinkers: Emerson, Thoreau, Alcott, Fuller, Longfellow, Lowell. The furtive writing of poetry must have seemed a selfish and overly ambitious preoccupation, especially in light of his bleak prospects for success at any task.

The story now, a hundred years after Frost's birth in San Francisco, needs no further embellishment to amaze us. That story in itself is a poem, as he would later see and pull together as his first book of poems, *A Boy's Will*, for which he composed notes to explain as much for himself as for the reader what he could finally recognize and enunciate, that "he will be rather more than less himself for having forsworn the world."[1] He would give all to love, or poetry, and go the way of the poet, the artist, as he had always reckoned himself to be.

Today Robert Frost is arguably the most popular and most respected American poet of the twentieth century, though sometimes for the wrong reasons. That assertion is, by itself, high praise for any writer, and is a major part of the complexity-beyond-simplicity Frost factored in to his poems, the "ulteriority" he often cautioned about. Even the most facile overview of biographical studies – Lawrance Thompson's three-volume monument[2] constructed on sand, William H. Pritchard's deft and quiet "reconsideration,"[3] Robert S. Newdick's unmanageable notes for a book[4], Wade Van Dore's indignant defense of the Leviathan[5] – reveals a mercurial spirit as intractable as a pebble of white quartz just beyond reach at the bottom of a well just close enough to reveal it, yet far away enough to tantalize us ceaselessly.

Or is it only a pebble? Could it be the "truth," after all? Certainly it is something more than merely "me myself in a shining surface picture," as he says in "For Once, Then, Something." The problem we have had and continue to have lies in Frost's deliberate construction of himself with his work. This is more artful and deceptive than a simple "persona" like Twain's or Emily Dickinson's. Here is truly a case where an artist has become one with his work, as poetry transformed Walt Whitman from a hack journalist into the other great American poet.

From the beginning, from the title of his very first book, *A Boy's Will*, Frost determined to take the cloak, if not the mantle, of Henry Wadsworth Longfellow. Schoolchildren by the scores of thousands had memorized "Tell me not in mournful numbers . . ." or had been mesmerized by the cadences of *Hiawatha*, that vanished red. Now Frost takes up the nostalgic "A boy's will is the wind's will/And the thoughts of youth are long, long thoughts," without open attribution, but because it is there for him, and us, to find. In Longfellow's response to American life and his dedication to form and structure in poetry, Frost doubtless found much of his own strength. Longfellow's "religious" sonnets, in Petrarchan form, are as good as many sonnets ever written in Britain or America. Surely a master craftsman like Frost observed Longfellow's sublimities and his falterings.

Frost's artfulness, perhaps the premier illustration of literary prescience, is then immediately revealed in the epigraph to *A Boy's Will*, which announces a constant metaphor in the poems and is the guiding principle of his intention as poet: to provide, as gravity clarifies a muddied spring, an instantaneous clarification of life or of doubt, "a momentary stay against confusion." The metaphor culminates Frost's career in *In the Clearing*, the successfulness of which is still debatable, as spring water may be murked in winter, or over time.

The figure is the same for poetry. The water image may inhere in other natural forms, as "ice on a hot stove riding on its own melting," or snow, or rain. Water itself may resist clarification. Or it may await the clarifier. This is the task of the scholar or critic. The reward is the cup from the playhouse at the top of the mountain in "Directive." The children and the playhouse have long since vanished, as has everything else but memory in that poem, and so the cup, like the grail, is purely symbolic and fantastic. Nevertheless a stay, a reprieve, is proffered. A very difficult, possibly distasteful, poem has been concluded; only the reader can decide whether the trek up the mountain was worthwhile, was worth the imaginary little drink of water.

For the critic, even such a structurally perfect and exquisite poem as "Stopping by Woods on a Snowy Evening" is open to wide-ranging debate. One critic below has determined that it is not one of Frost's best poems,[6] another that it is "indispensable" in considering Frost's work as a whole.[7] Yet to a casual reader the poem seems to suggest nothing more than that someone, otherwise hurried and fretful, pauses to witness the snow falling and to relish the moment, borrowed from time and swiped from the legal landholder. The decision to stop is an act of thought and will, which even the horse seems to find an unnatural variance from the routine. The man acknowledges that "the woods are lovely, dark and deep," which could signify death, or at least a deep slumber. Or the words could merely describe the actual scene. The setting *is* lovely. The woods *are* dark, for this is "the darkest evening of the year," whether meteorologically or psychologically. The woods are deep, because they are thick, packed New England woods, practically impenetrable. And yet the poet has set forth the possibility of symbolic meanings in his woods, his darkness, and his snow. He has very artfully drawn us into complexity, whether it is really there or not. Perhaps he knew that that was just enough, that no one would perceive the horse as anything but a horse or the lake as anything but a lake. Perhaps, too, the woods are too seductive to withstand, even in the face of the speaker's conclusion that there are "miles to go before" anything really changes. The poem, then, is an elephant-trap, and we can hardly avoid falling.

The critical tree consequently has branched in at least five directions since the poem first appeared in 1923. The most obvious way to interpret "Stopping by Woods" is the simplest, although "simple" is a word with lurking dangers in dealing with poetry. To be simple is not necessarily to be simple-minded, and no one has ever accused Robert Frost of that. But as a straightforward description of event and mood, as just provided, the poem evokes a sense of serenity and sympathy, an inner epiphany, a momentary stay against overwhelming darkness, real or imagined. And it lasts for just a moment, only long enough for the horse to become impatient, jarring the speaker back to responsibility.

On the other hand, it may be pointed out that the dominant impression is of darkness and not coldness. It is snowing and the lake is frozen, the only indications of winter. Darkness – "the darkest evening of the year" (usually December 23) – dominates the poem, leading John Ciardi in 1958[8] to point out the "death-wish" possibilities in the image of the dark, deep woods. Such an interpretation was inevitable because of the deceptive arrangement of the poem's materials, as Ciardi acknowledged, and because of the tendency, common to casual readers, to categorize or pigeonhole what is read into comfortable groups with easy referents, as undergraduate English majors can label anything ever written as ultimately about death. The symbol is in the eye of the beholder, whether one is Freudian, Jungian, Nietzschean, Marxist, or some other. Frost has shown us once more how far we can get into our own confusion and why we need so often to be extricated from it.

Still another field of pursuit which Frost's poetry engenders is that of source-hunting. Critics have found echoes or direct influences on "Stopping by Woods" in such divergent sources as Dante,[9] Indian proverbs,[10] and Thomas Lovell Beddoes.[11] Frost's reading is well-documented in the biographies and his own comments in letters and conversations. All speculation on his possible borrowings should demonstrate artistic genius at play in the Pantheon of "the Tradition," as T.S. Eliot referred to it. Frost as American poet is the imaginative maker of his world, adding to himself, as Whitman did, all things seen, read, or merely dreamed. To him all things are the grist of the imagination. No artist can deny the pervasive and enduring Shakespeare, the King James Bible,[12] or the best (and worst) of the English Romantic poets. Therefore, whether Frost borrowed from, or merely coincided with, another writer would seem to be merely curious and interesting.

In that same vein, it is illuminating to find parallels in Frost's philosophical thinking to such philosophers as Ralph Waldo Emerson, William James, and Henri Bergson,[13] who were major influences on the themes and attitudes in many of Frost's poems. As their ideas helped to inform the poetry, so they continue to aid in enlightened interpretation of individual poems. Again, a cautionary word is necessary so that Frost is seen not merely as a spokesman for a philosophical point of view, but is correctly observed as extrapolating the concepts and attitudes of thought which he has already intuited and could have enunciated without the acquaintance which nonetheless made it easier for him. Besides, as Ralph Waldo Emerson remarked, "We are as much informed of a writer's genius by what he selects as by what he originates."[14] What follows in this compilation is the record of scholarship: criticism, memoirs, recognition in popular journals, doctoral studies, appreciations, and biographies appearing during and after the centennial year of Frost's birth. Some poem titles are included as well, most of them admiring and a few in the sincerest flattery, imitative parody. The great bulk of writing occurred in 1974, as one would expect, nearly a hundred articles and books published all across the country and abroad. A rapid skimming of titles will suggest a disparate and fragmented variety of viewpoints on the single subject: Robert Frost and his poetry. Yet scrutiny reveals a clearing-up, a coming into focus, of perception, gradual but as revealing as the spring thaw in Vermont or New Hampshire.

The most significant scholarly production of 1974 is the volume of essays on Frost that appeared from the University Press of Mississippi. Jac Tharpe and others of the University of Southern Mississippi achieved a timely and fitting tribute, and provided the vehicle for explication and commentary that will be a landmark in the Frost terrain for years to come. Other books and articles marked the centennial as well, and scholarly production has not slowed in the years since, including two more collections of criticism from Southern Mississippi.

The Robert Frost Society

In the late 1970s, The Robert Frost Society was conceived by Kathryn Gibbs Harris (Ph.D., Michigan State University), who published an occasional newsletter at her own expense and effort. Her attempt to establish a real organization of scholars and teachers was met with tepid enthusiasm until she aligned the Society with the Modern Language Association of America as an affiliated organization with meetings held during the annual convention of the MLA in December of each year. At those meetings, papers on Frost and the poetry were presented to increasingly large gatherings. The success of each session was due entirely to Kathryn Harris's foresight and enthusiasm, along with her management of logistics, bureaucratic details, and public relations.

At the MLA convention in 1982, aware of Kathryn Gibbs Harris' poor health, this writer, along with Marjorie Cook and Nancy Carol Joyner, agreed that the Robert Frost Society must be kept afloat and even bolstered, as had been the original hope of its founder and mainstay since its inception. Accordingly, and with the approval of Kathryn Gibbs Harris, the seat of the organization became the University of Maryland in College Park, with the financial assistance of the English Department. I drew up a constitution, a plan for a rotating executive committee, and assumed the role of director and editor of a semiannual newsletter. The democratic arrangement – borrowed freely from similar literary organizations, the Franz Kafka Society specifically – was established, with a well-qualified and talented group of officers representing a wide range of academic and other institutions. The new executive board included Marjorie Cook, Nancy Joyner, and me, along with Ronald Bieganowski, Mordecai Marcus, Robert Fleissner, and Philip Gerber. The chairman of the board has the responsibility for the program at MLA, and this process has continued since then.

In the 1986 meeting of the Society at the MLA convention in New York, the members present voted to move the locus of the organization to Winthrop College, to be headed by Earl J. Wilcox, a faithful and active participant in the Society from its earliest days. The Newsletter now appears from Clemson University in the pages of the *South Carolina Review*.

Today, support of the Robert Frost Society is enthusiastic in word and deed, and the ultimate aim of establishing a critical journal may eventually be realized. Other major American poets are already well represented by the *Walt Whitman Journal*, *Paideuma* (Ezra Pound), the *Wallace Stevens Journal*, the *Emerson Society Quarterly*, and others – all well deserved and serving necessary issues. A *Robert Frost Journal* (or *Review* or *Quarterly*) is a worthy and sensible culmination of the aspiration of the founder of the Robert Frost Society and of those who have worked to advance the study and appreciation of the poetry of Robert Frost in his own country.

Notes

1. For convenience, see William Pritchard's *Poems by Robert Frost: "A Boy's Will" and "North of Boston."* New American Library (New York: Signet Books, 1989), p. 25.

2. See item 1976.70.

3. See item 1984.33.

4. See item 1976.67.

5. See item 1986.9.

6. See item 1975.4.

7. See item 1982.23.

8. In "Robert Frost: The Way to the Poem," *Saturday Review* 41 (12 April 1958): 13-15, 65.

9. 1979.43.

10. 1982.50.

11. 1978.47.

12. 1979.28.

13. 1978.26, 1976.22, 1980.2, 1983.2.

14. "Quotation and Originality," in *Complete Works of Emerson*, vol. 8, *Letters and Social Aims* (Boston: Houghton Mifflin, 1903-4), p. 178.

Writings about Robert Frost, 1974-1990

1974

1 ALLEN, MARGARET V. "'The Black Cottage': Robert Frost and the Jeffersonian Ideal of Equality." In *Frost: Centennial Essays*. Edited by Jac Tharpe. Jackson: University Press of Mississippi, pp. 221-29.

"Frost's political conservatism ... will at first suggest that Jeffersonian ideals in their undiluted form were too radical for him. Frost knew too much about the abuses of freedom to assent very readily to any abstract principles which lavished it indiscriminately on so many who used it so badly, so selfishly."

2 BACON, HELEN. "In- and Outdoor Schooling: Robert Frost and the Classics." *American Scholar* 43 (Fall): 640-49.

On Frost's education in the classical authors – Horace, Catullus, the Greek lyricists, and others – and influences on the poetry. Reprinted: 1975.21.

3 BALLANTINE, LESLEY FROST. Preface to *Robert Frost: A Descriptive Catalogue of Books and Manuscripts in the Clifton Waller Barrett Library, University of Virginia*. Charlottesville: University of Virginia Press, pp. ix-x.

Describes the Frosts' interest in collecting. Adds: "When awards are given for this remarkable compilation, one way of shaping the literary and personal life of Robert Frost, they will include the dedicated staff of the University of Virginia's rare archives."

4 BARRETT, C[LIFTON] WALLER. "On Collecting Robert Frost." In *Robert Frost: A Descriptive Catalogue of Books and Manuscripts in the*

1974

Clifton Waller Barrett Library, University of Virginia. Charlottesville: University of Virginia Press, pp. ix-xvii.

The collector describes the history and growth of his collection of Frost material, one of one thousand single-author collections.

5 BASLER, ROY P. "Robert Frost: Lobbyist for the Arts." *Quarterly Journal of the Library of Congress* 31 (April): 108-15.

Reprints in facsimile form the reading text with autograph revisions and corrections of the poem "Dedication," read at the inauguration of President John F. Kennedy.

6 BOOTH, EARL WALTER. "New England Quartet: E.A. Robinson, Robert Frost, Charles Ives, and Carl Ruggles." *DAI* 35, 03A, p. 1648. Ph.D. dissertation, University of Utah, 211 pp.

Compares poets Frost and Robinson and music composers Ives and Ruggles. Sees Emersonian transcendentalism in all four.

7 BOURDETTE, ROBERT E., Jr., and MICHAEL M. COHEN. "Frost's 'Aim' and the Problem of Interpretation." *English Record* (New York State English Council) 25 (Spring): 53-63.

Discusses "The Aim Was Song" as a vehicle for class discussion and teaching the elements involved in interpretations of poetry.

8 BROWN, MARICE C. "The Quest for 'all creatures great and small.'" In *Frost: Centennial Essays*. Edited by Jac Tharpe. Jackson: University Press of Mississippi, pp. 3-11.

Introduction to essays sponsored by the Committee on the Frost Centennial, University of Southern Mississippi, on the one-hundredth anniversary of Frost's birth. Essay concludes that Frost is universal, unlimited as to space or time.

9 CALHOUN, RICHARD J. "Frost in the Carolinas." *South Carolina Review* 7 (November): 3-12.

An unpublished talk given by Robert Frost at the University of North Carolina, Spring, 1957. Frost says: "One definition of a poem might be: it's run out of luck. It would be a good figure for it. Another one. There used to be an event in the track meet, I think, called the hop, skip, and jump. And the jump was the thing you hoped to do best in, I think. You get going, you know, and get up your momentum. And that last jump ought to be the finish off to it." Reads poems including "The Road Not Taken," "The Tuft of Flowers," "The Drumlin Woodchuck," "Once by the Pacific," "Departmental," and "Kitty Hawk."

10 CARMICHAEL, CHARLES. "Robert Frost as Romantic." In *Frost: Centennial Essays*. Edited by Jac Tharpe. Jackson: University Press of Mississippi, pp. 147-65.

"Frost's situation was the Romantic's: he experienced profound despair, alienation, and isolation early in his life, and his work in the widest sense was the continuous creation and destruction of a sense of value." He is a Byronic hero, a poet-visionary, which is reflected in the later poetry, to its detriment.

11 CHABOT, C. BARRY. "The 'Melancholy Dualism' of Robert Frost." *Review of Existential Psychology and Psychiatry* 13, no. 1:42-56.

Attempts to "understand Frost's wilderness psychologically . . . to locate the generating conflicts in his poetry not between man and the wilderness, but between man and those who people the wilderness and give it its terror – other men." Concludes that Frost stays a profoundly, sadly, private man, a man who could never trust either himself or his world enough to become "whole again beyond confusion."

12 CIFELLI, EDWARD. "Ciardi on Frost: An Interview." In *Frost: Centennial Essays*. Edited by Jac Tharpe. Jackson: University Press of Mississippi, pp. 471-95.

John Ciardi, poet and longtime editor of the *Saturday Review*, talks about the poetry and his friendship with the poet. Also comments on his famous "death-wish" analysis of "Stopping by Woods," which is still a provoking analysis. Concludes: "I think it's ridiculous to assume that Frost is simply a passionate man with certain darknesses and certain confusions in him. He was that, plus a master poet forever in the presence of his medium."

13 CLARKE, MARIAN G.M., comp. *The Robert Frost Collection in the Watkinson Library*. Hartford, Conn.: Trinity College, 104 pp.

Lists items resulting from the collections of H. Bacon Collamore and Charles R. Green, as well as additional gifts and purchases. "The unsegregated, chronological arrangement was adopted to bring related items together. The index sorts out categories."

14 COALE, SAMUEL. "The Emblematic Encounter of Robert Frost." In *Frost: Centennial Essays*. Edited by Jac Tharpe. Jackson: University Press of Mississippi, pp. 89-107.

"Frost's emblematic encounter with nature reveals the basic 'strategy' of his poetry. He celebrates the physical presence of natural facts and the integrity of action in man's relation to them . . . believing that to add too much meaning to them is finally to betray their own elusive and ultimately mysterious solidity, to take away the meaning of the actual encounter."

15 CONDER, JOHN J. "'After Apple-Picking': Frost's Troubled Sleep." In *Frost: Centennial Essays*. Edited by Jac Tharpe. Jackson: University Press of Mississippi, pp. 171-81.

"What *will* trouble the speaker's sleep, whatever sleep it is? He is only falling asleep in this poem, and he does not yet know which sleep his will be. Its duration will determine its nature. It is his uncertainty as to when (or whether) he will awaken which will be carried into his sleep, troubling it. Ironically enough, only when he awakens will he know what sleep it is–or, rather, was."

16 COOK, REGINALD L. "The Critics and Robert Frost." In *Frost: Centennial Essays*. Edited by Jac Tharpe. Jackson: University Press of Mississippi, pp. 15-30.

On Frost's struggle to gain recognition and approval from the critics, and the literary quarrels among them. "During the latter years we saw Frost chiefly as one who had survived a conspiring silence to pick his way through the pressing crowd of approbative *and* detractive critics in a personal triumphal march."

17 ____. *Robert Frost: A Living Voice*. Amherst: University of Massachusetts Press, 331 pp.

Attempts "in this series of interrelated essays, based on notes from 1925 until 1963 and on a number of tape recordings of the 1950s and early 1960s, to clarify directly by quotation and indirectly by personal insight what Frost's poetry meant to him and to those who receive it. In effect, the stress will be equally upon what Frost said and the way he said it."

18 ____. "Robert Frost: An Equilibrist's Field of Vision." *Massachusetts Review* 15 (Summer): 385-401.

On Frost's balancing of opposites in himself and in his poetry. Reprinted: 1974.17.

19 COX, JAMES M. "Robert Frost and the End of the New England Line." In *Frost: Centennial Essays*. Edited by Jac Tharpe. Jackson: University Press of Mississippi, pp. 545-61.

On how Frost is similar to, and different from, Emerson and Thoreau. "If Emerson had been the promise of New England, and Thoreau its pure but fiercely individual present, Frost was to be its memory, its tradition. ... Traditional lyric, dramatic, and pastoral forms are at last embodied by a genuine New England voice."

20 CRANE, JOAN St.C., comp. *Robert Frost: A Descriptive Catalogue of Books and Manuscripts in the Clifton Waller Barrett Library, University of Virginia*. Charlottesville: University of Virginia, 280 pp.

A descriptive bibliography listing books and pamphlets, Christmas cards, first appearances of prose and poetry in books and periodicals, and manuscripts and letters. Includes a useful index.

21 CROWLEY, J. DONALD. "Hawthorne and Frost: The Making of a Poem." In *Frost: Centennial Essays*. Edited by Jac Tharpe. Jackson: University Press of Mississippi, pp. 288-309.

Presents Hawthorne's *American Notebooks* as the source for Frost's "The Wood-Pile."

22 DAVISON, PETER. "Self-Realization of Robert Frost, 1911-1912." *New Republic* 170 (March 30): 17-20.

Remarks delivered at the Library of Congress 26 March 1974. Discusses Frost's discovery of himself as a poet in England at age 37. Reprinted: 1975.21.

23 DENDINGER, LLOYD N. "Emerson's Influence on Frost through Howells." In *Frost: Centennial Essays*. Edited by Jac Tharpe. Jackson: University Press of Mississippi, pp. 265-74.

"Frost's regionalism, his affinities with William Dean Howells and the prose realists, provided him with the means of making poetry of the materials of an age that was forcing upon other poets the decision to turn away from it, to turn backward in time to tradition or to turn inward to the creation of individual myth."

24 DICKEY, JOHN SLOAN. "Robert Frost: Glimpses of the Man." *Dartmouth College Library Bulletin* 15 (November): 2-5.

Prints a talk given by Dartmouth's President Emeritus at a program, "Afternoon with Robert Frost," held at Derry, N.H., on 26 March 1974, as part of the observance marking the centennial of the poet's birth and the issuance of a commemorative stamp in his honor. In his "resolute inner privacy" there was the "need to assert, at least to himself, his ultimate independence of both friend and foe."

25 DOYLE, JOHN ROBERT. *Sources of "West-Running Brook."* Charleston: Military College of South Carolina, 18 pp.

Cites the earliest source as the Greek Heraclitus (c. 536-475 B.C.).

26 EDWARDS, MARGARET. "Pan's Song, Revised: Robert Frost as the Articulate Backwoodsman." In *Frost: Centennial Essays*. Edited by Jac Tharpe. Jackson: University Press of Mississippi, pp. 108-20.

Frost rejects Emerson's view of nature with an "unsentimental view of the human urge to survive" in an increasingly technological world. "Frost encompasses this grim reality in his aesthetic and moral vision, and his poems collectively illustrate the possibility of a life in which man's struggle with nature fits within nature's larger harmonies."

27 EKINS, ROGER. "'At Home' with Robert Frost." In *Frost: Centennial Essays*. Edited by Jac Tharpe. Jackson: University Press of Mississippi, pp. 191-200.

On "home" as a metaphor in Frost's poetry. "He has used 'home' as shelter, as a means of creating cosmos out of chaos, and he has attempted to extend the dimensions of home to include Nature and even the universe."

28 EVANS, WILLIAM R. "A Literary Friendship: Robert Frost and Carl Burell." In *Frost: Centennial Essays*. Edited by Jac Tharpe. Jackson: University Press of Mississippi, pp. 504-17.

About the boyhood friends and Burell's early poetic influence on Frost. Although the friendship was not continued after Frost's fame began, Burell had been a significant force in Frost's becoming a poet.

29 FERGUSON, ALFRED R. "Frost and the Paradox of the Fortunate Fall." In *Frost: Centennial Essays*. Edited by Jac Tharpe. Jackson: University Press of Mississippi, pp. 427-40.

On Frost's metaphor of *felix culpa*, the connections between evil and good, between fate and choice, and the metaphors of Eden and the Fall.

30 FINNEGAN, SISTER MARY JEREMY. "Frost Remakes an Ancient Story." In *Frost: Centennial Essays*. Edited by Jac Tharpe. Jackson: University Press of Mississippi, pp. 389-97.

On Frost's *Hard Not to Be King* (New York: House of Books, 1951). [Originally, "How Hard It Is to Keep from Being King When It's in You and in the Situation," 1950.] Finds parallels in ancient Persian and Indian tales, though Frost has added psychological complexity.

31 FLEISSNER, ROBERT F. "Frost's 'Moon Compasses.'" *Explicator* 32 (May): Item 66.

Compares Frost's compass image to that in John Donne's "A Valediction: Forbidding Mourning."

32 _____. "Like 'Pythagoras' Comparison of the Universe with Number': A Frost-Tennyson Correlation." In *Frost: Centennial Essays*. Edited by Jac Tharpe. Jackson: University Press of Mississippi, pp. 207-20.

On the numbers three and five in Frost's "The Gold Hesperidee" and Tennyson's "The Hesperides."

33 FROST, LESLEY. "Certain Intensities." *Ball State University Forum* 15 (Summer): 3-8.

Recounts her father's comments on her mystery novel, *Murder at Large*: "Such good writing in the three or four kinds needed to build a novel: intensities of the imagined scene (you grew up on this); intensities of dialogue; intensities of insight into character and situation. Too good to be a detective novel." Includes cover photograph of Frost (Franconia, N.H., 1915) by Ellen Webster.

34 GAHAGAN, G. WILLIAM. "A 'Day' in the Life of Robert Lee Frost: 1874." In *Frost: Centennial Essays*. Edited by Jac Tharpe. Jackson: University Press of Mississippi, pp. 496-503.

Relates San Francisco newspaper accounts of events there and elsewhere around 26 March 1874, the day of Frost's birth. Frost is quoted as saying the location was "up on Washington Street in San Francisco on Nob Hill somewhere."

35 GARRISON, JOSEPH M., Jr. "'Our Singing Strength': The Texture of Voice in the Poetry of Robert Frost." In *Frost: Centennial Essays*. Edited by Jac Tharpe. Jackson: University Press of Mississippi, pp. 340-50.

Asserts that the ear, not just the eye, is essential to understanding Frost's prosody and thus his meaning.

36 GERBER, PHILIP L. "Robert Frost–2074 A.D." In *Frost: Centennial Essays*. Edited by Jac Tharpe. Jackson: University Press of Mississippi, pp. 31-41.

A whimsical survey of critical opinions of the past and projections into the twenty-first century. "The Frost canon of 2074 A.D.–what will it be when the Untermeyer of that age chooses what goes and what stays?"

1974

37 GREINER, DONALD J. *Robert Frost: The Poet and His Critics*. Chicago: American Library Association, 314 pp.

An interpretive prose bibliography. Includes an index to poems.

38 ____. "Robert Frost: The Poet as Critic: An Analysis and a Checklist." *South Carolina Review* 7 (November): 48-60.

Discusses Frost's shortcomings as a practical critic. Provides a bibliography of his critical prose, talks, interviews, letters, and memoirs about him.

39 ____. "Robert Frost's Dark Woods and the Function of Metaphor." In *Frost: Centennial Essays*. Edited by Jac Tharpe. Jackson: University Press of Mississippi, pp. 373-88.

On the variety of the woods metaphor in Frost's poetry, a metaphor which "shows how the true poet simultaneously recognizes something new in a common object, uses figurative language to suggest the correspondence, and demands that the reader be educated enough in poetry to pick up the unanticipated metaphorical notation."

40 ____. "'That Plain-Speaking Guy': A Conversation with James Dickey on Robert Frost." In *Frost: Centennial Essays*. Edited by Jac Tharpe. Jackson: University Press of Mississippi, pp. 51-59.

The interview was focused on "what makes Robert Frost a great poet and why his poems continue to invite serious reading." Frost speaks "plainly and deeply ... a plain speaking style which could say profound things." Dickey would choose "Acquainted with the Night" and "After Apple-Picking" for a "world anthology."

41 HANCHER, MICHAEL. "'Sermons in Stones': An Explication of Robert Frost's Poem 'A Missive Missile.'" *Centrum* 2 (Spring): 79-86.

Discusses this "hermeneutic parable" in which Frost aims "to undermine and satirize ... the poem's beguiled, sentimental, and sentimentalizing speaker."

42 HARRIS, KATHRYN GIBBS. "Robert Frost's Early Education in Science." *South Carolina Review* 7 (November): 13-33.

Describes Frost's early years and his reading in science from Carl Burell's library. Later he encountered the work of William James and Henri Bergson. He also remarked much later that his favorite journal was the *Scientific American*.

1974

43 HAYS, PETER L. "Two Landscapes: Frost's and Eliot's" In *Frost: Centennial Essays*. Edited by Jac Tharpe. Jackson: University Press of Mississippi, pp. 256-64.

Suggests that Frost's notes to *New Hampshire* may satirize Eliot's notes to "The Waste Land." Also: "I believe he structured *New Hampshire* as he did, not only to mock Eliot's pedantry and "obscuration," but also to counter Eliot's pervasive pessimistic tone."

44 HENRY, NAT. "Frost's 'Stopping by Woods on a Snowy Evening.'" *Explicator* 32 (January): Item 33.

Objects to John Ciardi's controversial interpretation of the poem as about a "death wish."

45 HOPKINS, VIVIAN C. "The Houses of Robert Frost." In *Frost: Centennial Essays*. Edited by Jac Tharpe. Jackson: University Press of Mississippi, pp. 182-90.

Describes several of the houses the Frosts lived in in this country and England and the metaphorical significance of house and home in the poetry.

46 KANTAK, V.Y. "Poetic Ambiguity in Frost." *Western Humanities Review* 28 (Winter): 31-46.

Discusses the variety of methods Frost uses to achieve the "so-called 'evasiveness' of his poetry."

47 KERNAN, MICHAEL. "Remembering the Young Robert Frost: 'Waiting in Irritable Obscurity.'" *Washington Post*, 27 March, Section B, p. 2.

Reviews talks given at the Library of Congress on Frost by Robert Pack, Allen Tate, Peter Davison, and Helen H. Bacon.

48 LATHEM, EDWARD CONNERY. Introduction to *Robert Frost's Tribute to E.A. Robinson: From the Introduction to "King Jasper."* Boston: David R. Godine, pp. [4-6].

Describes the background that elicited Frost's comment. Photostat reproduction of Frost's holograph copy of the essay for Robinson's publisher.

49 ____, comp. *Robert Frost 100*. Boston: David R. Godine, 104 pp.

Lists 100 items of Frost's publications assembled for a traveling exhibit in the United States from May to December 1974.

1974

50 LENTRICCHIA, FRANK. "Robert Frost and Modern Literary Theory." In *Frost: Centennial Essays*. Edited by Jac Tharpe. Jackson: University Press of Mississippi, pp. 315-32.

Frost is more "modern" than usually supposed. His philosophical and epistemological pragmatism derives from William James and is the bridge from his Kantian Romanticism, creating the "landscape" of the poems. Analyzes "All Revelation" in this light.

51 LINDNER, CARL M. "Robert Frost: 'In the American Grain.'" *Colorado Quarterly* 22 (Fall): 469-79.

Discusses Frost's "Americanness" by showing similarities to Emerson, Thoreau, and Melville.

52 LINEBARGER, J.M. "Sources of Frost's 'The Vindictives.'" *American Notes & Queries* 12 (May-June): 150-54.

Finds Frost's source to be a combination of William H. Prescott's *Conquest of Peru* and *The Conquest of Mexico*.

53 LITTLEJOHN, DAVID. "Frost at 100: Still on Tour." *New Republic* 171 (16 November): 23-24.

A tribute for Frost's centennial. Discusses "La Noche Triste."

54 LYNEN, JOHN F. "Du Côté de Chez Frost." In *Frost: Centennial Essays*. Edited by Jac Tharpe. Jackson: University Press of Mississippi, pp. 562-94.

Describes several varieties of the modernity of Frost, using "Directive" as a frame of reference.

55 MARTIN, JUDITH. "Robert Frost Centennial." *Washington Post*, 26 March, Section C, p. 2.

Lists various events in Washington and elsewhere during the year which marks 100 years since Frost's birth. Also describes a new Robert Frost commemorative postage stamp, one of the American Poets series, to be issued at Derry, N.H.

56 MASSEY, WAYNE DOUGLAS. "Aspects of Darkness in the Poetry of Robert Frost." *DAI* 35, 03A, p. 1629. Ph.D. dissertation, Ball State University, 127 pp.

Examines Frost's methods for dealing with various sorts of "darkness": the hardships and fears of the poet himself, the dark elements of the human condition, and natural darkness.

1974

57 MILLER, LEWIS H., Jr. "Design and Drama in *A Boy's Will*." In *Frost: Centennial Essays*. Edited by Jac Tharpe. Jackson: University Press of Mississippi, pp. 351-68.

"The design of *A Boy's Will* is both thematic and dramatic, and it is unique to the Frost canon in its portrayal of a young, often immature speaker who develops and ripens as the poems unfold. At the same time, there are several thematic strands in *A Boy's Will* which prefigure the dynamics of later, more mature volumes. Thus, Frost's first volume can be viewed as both a proving ground for the Frost with whom we are perhaps most familiar and as a poetic accomplishment in its own right of close examination."

58 ____. "The Poet as Swinger: Fact and Fancy in Robert Frost." *Criticism* 16 (Winter): 58-72.

Discusses "Birches," "Mowing," and "The Wood-Pile" to illustrate Frost's poetic strategy in dealing with the problem "How to do justice to a chaotic, viscously contingent reality, and yet redeem it?"

59 MONTEIRO, GEORGE. "Robert Frost's Metaphysical Sonnet." In *Frost Centennial Essays*. Edited by Jac Tharpe. Jackson: University Press of Mississippi, pp. 333-39.

On the writing of "Design," from the first manuscript form to the final published version, revealing Frost's consistency of purpose.

60 ____. "Unlinked Myth in Frost's 'Mending Wall.'" *Concerning Poetry* 7 (Fall): 10-11.

Suggests that the poem stops short of the mythological link of Terminus, the Roman god of boundaries, and does not affirm boundaries at all.

61 MORRISON, KATHLEEN. *Robert Frost: A Pictorial Chronicle*. New York: Holt, Rinehart and Winston, 133 pp.

An affectionate reminiscence with seventy-eight photographs. Sensitive and well-written, it describes her relationship with Frost as his secretary and confidante after his wife's death in 1938.

62 NITCHIE, GEORGE W. "Robert Frost: The Imperfect Guru." In *Frost: Centennial Essays*. Edited by Jac Tharpe. Jackson: University Press of Mississippi, pp. 42-50.

"As thinker or as guru . . . Frost must be taken with a great deal of caution. There's a real romantic nihilist in him, and romantic nihilists may be exciting, but they make dangerous intellectual and moral guides, especially when they seem to present themselves in the guise of Burkean conservatives."

63 PERRINE, LAURENCE. "The Meaning of Frost's 'Build Soil.'" In *Frost: Centennial Essays*. Edited by Jac Tharpe. Jackson: University Press of Mississippi, pp. 230-35.

"Just as the building of good soil is necessary for the production of healthy and abundant crops, Tityrus argues, so the development of a rich individuality in human beings is necessary for writing good poetry. The great danger of modern life is that we rush into the social arena too fast, take our crops to market too soon. We desperately need to 'build soil,' to practice self-cultivation more intensely."

64 ____. "The Sense of Frost's 'The Self-Seeker.'" *Concerning Poetry* 7 (Fall): 5-8.

Suggests three meanings for the poem: that the title is ironical; that, in a deeper sense, it is literal; or that it is partly literal, partly ironic.

65 POIRIER, RICHARD. "The Sound of Love and the Love of Sound." *Atlantic Monthly* 233 (April): 50-55.

Suggests that, because of his popularity, Frost "has become a kind of embarrassment to those who would recognize his greatness." Attempts to show why "his genius is so hard to account for."

66 RECHNITZ, ROBERT M. "The Tragic Vision of Robert Frost." In *Frost: Centennial Essays*. Edited by Jac Tharpe. Jackson: University Press of Mississippi, pp. 133-46.

"Frost possesses a tragic vision. . . . Yet behind almost all of Frost's poems we sense a belief in the magnitude of man, and we detect in Frost's thought a sense of heroism of which every man partakes by the simple process of living out his life."

67 REICHERT, VICTOR E. "The Faith of Robert Frost." In *Frost: Centennial Essays*. Edited by Jac Tharpe. Jackson: University Press of Mississippi, pp. 415-26.

Rabbi Reichert describes aspects of his friendship with Frost, focusing on religious interests. Frost was "Old Testament Biblical and Hebrew prophetic," a perceptive reader of the Scripture.

68 "Robert Lee Frost: A Taste for Irony, an Aptitude for Style, 'And Miles to Go. . . .'" *Washington Post*, 26 March, Section C, pp. 1, 2.

Describes Frost's involvement in the inauguration of President John F. Kennedy.

69 RODMAN, SELDEN. "Robert Frost." In *Tongues of Fallen Angels*. New York: New Directions Publishers, pp. 38-49.

Describes a visit with Frost in Ripton, Vermont, in 1949. Frost concludes: "Happiness is a mirage. My life has taught me that much, or that little – look at what happened to my family, but I won't go into *that*. Wine, women, and song can be pursued and won. And the song – the poetry – must be soft but not flabby, hard but not like nails."

70 ROSEN, KENNETH. "Visions and Revisions: An Early Version of Robert Frost's 'Our Doom to Bloom.'" In *Frost: Centennial Essays*. Edited by Jac Tharpe. Jackson: University Press of Mississippi, pp. 369-72.

Describes a holograph version of the poem in a letter at the Boyd Lee Spahr Library at Dickinson College. Compares the early version with the published one.

71 SANDERS, DAVID A. "Smokeless Burning: Imagination and Survival in the Poetry of Robert Frost." *DAI* 35, 06A, p. 3767. Ph.D. dissertation, Cornell University, 232 pp.

Examines the theme of nature as a continuous process of dissolution. "Nature works to assimilate man to itself, to make man's body earth again. In resisting that pull – in his life and art – he tries to make the world embody imagination." Uses "The Wood-Pile" as the primary focus of the argument.

72 ____. "Words in the Rush of Everything to Waste: A Poetic Theme in Frost." *South Carolina Review* 7 (November): 34-47.

Suggests that Frost's nature lyrics reveal his "tactic for imaginative survival" stemming from an "effort to save what we value from the temporal current that threatens to bear everything away."

73 SCHUTZ, FRED C. "Frost's 'The Literate Farmer and the Planet Venus': Why 1926?" *Notes on Contemporary Literature* 4 (November): 8-11.

Suggests that Frost chose 1926 because of events in the life of Thomas A. Edison and his invention, the electric light bulb.

74 ____. "Frost's 'The Witch of Coös.'" *Explicator* 33 (November): Item 19.

"The limited verifications made by the narrator do accomplish Frost's purpose: the reader is made to conclude, from his study of the multiple and conflicting refractions of narrator, witch, son, and Toffile, that the story offers more problems than answers."

75 SHURR, WILLIAM H. "Once More to the 'Woods': A New Point of Entry into Frost's Most Famous Poem." *New England Quarterly* 47 (December): 584-94.

The "new point" is the climactic phrase "A deep but dazzling darkness" in Henry Vaughan's "The Night."

76 SKOW, JOHN. "The Roads Taken." *Time* 104 (12 August): 74.

Review of 1974.61. Sees Morrison as "a protector in her recollections, which favor Frost and reticence . . . who thought his pouts and tantrums worth putting up with, and who conspired elaborately to ease him through the last half of his life."

77 STAFFORD, WILLIAM. "The Terror in Robert Frost." *New York Times Magazine*, 18 August, pp. 24-26, 31, 33, 35, 37-38.

On Frost's sometimes intemperate behavior and his "dark side."

78 STAMPER, REXFORD. "Robert Frost: An Assessment of Criticism, Realism, and Modernity." In *Frost: Centennial Essays*. Edited by Jac Tharpe. Jackson: University Press of Mississippi, pp. 60-86.

Provides an overview of the major critical evaluations of the poetry. Frost is concerned with the same problems as Eliot and Yeats, but he created "his own verities." Frost is "a major twentieth-century artist."

79 STANLIS, PETER J. "Robert Frost's Masques and the Classic American Tradition." In *Frost: Centennial Essays*. Edited by Jac Tharpe. Jackson: University Press of Mississippi, pp. 441-68.

Discusses the masques as Frost's serious attempts to the relationship between God and man. Frost's approach is thoroughly "American."

80 STEGNER, WALLACE. *The Uneasy Chair: A Biography of Bernard DeVoto*. Garden City, N.Y.: Doubleday & Co., 464 pp.

Describes the relationship with Frost, passim, and their quarrel and breakup at Bread Loaf in 1938. Includes index.

81 STONE, EDWARD. "Other 'Desert Places': Frost and Hawthorne." In *Frost: Centennial Essays*. Edited by Jac Tharpe. Jackson: University Press of Mississippi, pp. 275-87.

Frost's choice of *desert* seems archaic and untypical of him. His source for the word and its specific meanings may be in Hawthorne, especially *The Scarlet Letter*. See also 1974.21.

82 THARPE, JAC L. "Frost as Representative of the Eidolons." In *Frost: Centennial Essays*. Edited by Jac Tharpe. Jackson: University Press of Mississippi, pp. 595-606.

As a representative of America, as for example during his trip to Russia, Frost embodies Walt Whitman's use of the term *eidolon*, meaning the myths or verities of the United States.

83 ____, ed. *Frost: Centennial Essays*. Jackson: University Press of Mississippi, 610 pp.

Contents: Marice C. Brown, "The Quest for 'All Creatures Great and Small'"; J[ac] T[harpe], "Achievement"; Reginald L. Cook, "The Critics and Robert Frost"; Philip L. Gerber, "Robert Frost–2074 A.D."; George W. Nitchie, "Robert Frost: The Imperfect Guru"; Donald J. Greiner, "'That Plain-Speaking Guy': A Conversation with James Dickey on Robert Frost"; Rexford Stamper, "Robert Frost: An Assessment of Criticism, Realism, and Modernity"; D[avid] B[rown], "Nature"; Samuel Coale, "The Emblematic Encounter of Robert Frost"; Margaret Edwards, "Pan's Song, Revised: Robert Frost as the Articulate Backwoodsman"; Albert J. Von Frank, "'Nothing That Is': A Study of Frost's 'Desert Places'"; Robert M. Rechnitz, "The Tragic Vision of Robert Frost"; Charles Carmichael, "Robert Frost as a Romantic"; P[eggy] W. P[renshaw], "Themes"; John J. Conder, "'After Apple-Picking': Frost's Troubled Sleep"; Vivian C. Hopkins, "The Houses of Robert Frost"; Roger Ekins, "'At Home' with Robert Frost"; Nancy Vogel, "A Post Mortem on 'The Death of the Hired Man'"; Robert F. Fleissner, "Like 'Pythagoras' Comparison of the Universe with Number': A Frost-Tennyson Correlation"; Margaret V. Allen, "'The Black Cottage': Robert Frost and the Jeffersonian Ideal of Equality"; Laurence Perrine, "The Meaning of Frost's 'Build Soil'"; J[ac] T[harpe], "Contexts"; Perry D. Westbrook, "Robert Frost's New England"; Peter L. Hays, "Two Landscapes: Frost's and Eliot's"; Lloyd N. Dendinger, "Emerson's Influence on Frost Through Howells"; Edward Stone, "Other 'Desert Places': Frost and Hawthorne"; J. Donald Crowley, "Hawthorne and Frost: The Making of a Poem"; G[ordon] W[eaver], "Method and Theory"; Frank Lentricchia, "Robert Frost and Modern Literary Theory"; George Monteiro, "Robert Frost's

Metaphysical Sonnet"; Joseph M. Garrison, Jr., "'Our Singing Strength': The Texture of Voice in the Poetry of Robert Frost"; Lewis H. Miller, Jr., "Design and Drama in *A Boy's Will*"; Kenneth Rosen, "Visions and Revisions: An Early Version of Robert Frost's 'Our Doom to Bloom'"; Donald J. Greiner, "Robert Frost's Dark Woods and the Function of Metaphor"; Sister Mary Jeremy Finnegan, "Frost Remakes an Ancient Story"; Stephen D. Warner, "Robert Frost in the Clearing: The Risk of Spirit in Substantiation"; J[ac] T[harpe], "Religion"; Victor E. Reichert, "The Faith of Robert Frost"; Alfred R. Ferguson, "Frost and the Paradox of the Fortunate Fall"; Peter J. Stanlis, "Robert Frost's Masques and the Classic American Tradition"; J[ac] T[harpe], "Biography and Reminiscence"; Edward Cifelli, "Ciardi on Frost: An Interview"; G. William Gahagan, "A 'Day' in the Life of Robert Lee Frost–1874"; William R. Evans, "A Literary Friendship: Robert Frost and Carl Burell"; Dorothy Tyler, "Frost's Last Three Visits to Michigan"; Wade Van Dore, "The Subtlety of Robert Frost"; J[ac] T[harpe], "Robert Frost"; James M. Cox, "Robert Frost and the End of the New England Line"; John F. Lynen, "Du Côté de Chez Frost"; Jac L. Tharpe, "Afterword: Frost as Representative of the Eidolons."

84 THOMPSON, SUSAN. "Boundaries of the Self: Poetry by Frost, Roethke, and Berryman, Considered in the Light of the Language of Schizophrenia." *DAI* 35, 08A, p. 5430. Ph.D. dissertation, University of Texas, 173 pp.

Sees evidence of schizophrenic language patterns in "Mending Wall," "Desert Places," "The Witch of Coös," and "A Servant to Servants."

85 TOWER, SAMUEL T. "Robert Frost–American Poet." *New York Times*, 24 February, Section D, p. 28.

Announces the new ten-cent Frost commemorative stamp. Describes Frost's significance.

86 TYLER, DOROTHY. "Frost's Last Three Visits to Michigan." In *Frost: Centennial Essays*. Edited by Jac Tharpe. Jackson: University Press of Mississippi, pp. 511-34.

Affectionate reminiscences of Frost in Ann Arbor, from materials for a projected book to be called *Robert Frost in Michigan*. Describes conversations, readings, and other appearances and the adulation of his admirers.

1974

87 VAIL, DENNIS. "Frost's 'Mowing': Work and Poetry." *Notes on Contemporary Literature* 4 (January): 4-8.

Suggests that the poem is about the work of poetry. It "embodies an especially vivid image of the purity, discipline and paradoxically disinterested passion that, at least for Frost, identify the artist's act."

88 ____. "Point of View in Frost's 'The Peaceful Shepherd.'" *Notes on Contemporary Literature* 4 (January): 2-4.

Finds that "the poem points the way from a certain attractive but limited peacefulness, which is bound to end somehow in frustration, bewilderment and disarray, toward that true peace that is the peace of reconcilement."

89 VAN EGMOND, PETER. *The Critical Reception of Robert Frost*. Boston: G.K. Hall, 319 pp.

Provides an annotated checklist of secondary material on Frost, including books, articles, interviews, anthologies, poems to or about Frost, news items, and doctoral dissertations through 1973.

90 VITELLI, JAMES R. "Robert Frost: The Contrarieties of Talent and Tradition." *New England Quarterly* 47 (September): 351-67.

Sees Frost as a difficult and contrary poet, yet a popular one. His designs put him above the contrarieties of the American tradition.

91 VOGEL, NANCY. "A Post Mortem on 'The Death of the Hired Man.'" In *Frost: Centennial Essays*. Edited by Jac Tharpe. Jackson: University Press of Mississippi, pp. 201-6.

On the language devices and themes in the poem.

92 ____. *Robert Frost, Teacher*. Bloomington, Ind.: Phi Delta Kappa, 99 pp.

Examines Frost's love-hate relationship with schools and schooling. Discusses Frost as a teacher and his methods in the classroom and with students.

93 VON FRANK, ALBERT J. "'Nothing That Is': A Study of Frost's 'Desert Places.'" In *Frost: Centennial Essays*. Edited by Jac Tharpe. Jackson: University Press of Mississippi, pp. 121-32.

"The despair of 'Desert Places,' then, consists most simply in the recognition of the limits of the mind. The freedom which it expresses is the paradoxical counterpoint to the despair and consists in the recognition that the mind is essentially *un*limited."

1974

94 WARNER, STEPHEN D. "Robert Frost in the Clearing: The Risk of Spirit in Substantiation." In *Frost: Centennial Essays*. Edited by Jac Tharpe. Jackson: University Press of Mississippi, pp. 398-411.

Frost's final volume completes the personal cycle begun in *A Boy's Will* and reveals "a new confidence reflected through the tone and statement of the poems." Analyzes the poems in comparison with previous ones with similar themes.

95 WATKINS, FLOYD C. "Going and Coming Back: Robert Frost's Religious Poetry." *South Atlantic Quarterly* 73 (Autumn): 445-59.

Argues that "Frost was never able to write a poem at a moment of intense belief–if he had such moments. Without exception, I believe, his good poems come in the shadows of yearnings and doubts. His great lyric and dramatic poems never place much confidence in nature or in God."

96 WESTBROOK, PERRY D. "Robert Frost's New England." In *Frost: Centennial Essays*. Edited by Jac Tharpe. Jackson: University Press of Mississippi, pp. 239-55.

Although not a native New Englander, Frost's attitudes were shaped by the social and cultural conditions of rural New England, especially as a farmer at Derry, New Hampshire, between 1900 and 1906. Sees a kinship with other New England writers of that time, although his work transcends that of the local-color writers."

1975

1 BARRETT, CLIFTON WALLER. "*Twilight*: Robert Frost's First Book" In *Proof, 4: The Yearbook of American Bibliographical and Textual Studies*. Edited by Joseph Katz. Columbia, S.C.: J. Faust & Co., pp. 3-5.

Introduces a facsimile reproduction of the unique copy of Frost's first book of poetry (1894, pp. 6-21). By the well-known collector of literary materials and benefactor of the Clifton Waller Barrett Library, University of Virginia, Charlottesville.

2 BLEICH, DAVID. "Robert Frost and Cultural Popularity." *Sphinx* 3:21-40.

Describes the popular perception of Frost as a "benign" figure and the conflicting reports of Frost as vindictive and mean.

3 BORKAT, ROBERTA F. SARFATT. "The Bleak Landscape of Robert Frost." *Midwest Quarterly* 16 (July): 453-67.

Shows the complexity of the bleak poetic world depicted in the two masques of Frost.

4 CARRUTH, HAYDEN. "Robert Frost." *Parnassus* 3 (Spring-Summer): 35-41.

Review article on Lathem and Thompson, *Collected Poems*. Finds "'Stopping by Woods . . . ' not Frost's best poem. Probably his best are his long ones." Suggests further that some poems are forced or even "faked."

5 COLLINS, MICHAEL J. "A Note on Frost's 'Love and a Question.'" *Concerning Poetry* 8 (Spring): 57-58.

Reply to 1972.2. Suggests that there is no dilemma in the poem.

6 COOK, MARJORIE. "The Complexity of Boundaries: 'Trespass' by Robert Frost." *Notes on Contemporary Literature* 5 (Fall): 2-5.

Examines the irony of supposed property rights in the poem and the possible influence of Emerson's "Hamatreya."

7 CRANE, JOAN St.C. "The Printing History of *Twilight*." *Proof, 4: The Yearbook of American Bibliographical and Textual Studies*. Edited by Joseph Katz. Columbia, S.C.: J. Faust & Co., pp. 22-30.

Reproduces, in facsimile, the commencement program of Lawrence (Mass.) High School. Describes Frost's dealings with the American Printing House, probable printer of *Twilight*.

8 DJOS, MATTS GILMAN. "The Polarities and Fusions of Loneliness and Severity and of Decay and Renewal in the Poetry of Robert Frost." *DAI* 36, 07A, p. 5294. Ph.D. dissertation, Texas A&M, 159 pp.

Examines various polarities in Frost's poetry. Concludes: "Life simultaneously runs down and recreates itself; severity and beauty are ultimately all-encompassing components of a final vision of natural order; and the flux of regeneration is paradoxically reflected in a pattern that is static and inalterable."

9 EBERHART, RICHARD. "Robert Frost in the Clearing." *Southern Review* 11 (April): 260-68.

Reminiscence of a long acquaintance with Frost. Concludes: "As to his thinking, Frost is the only poet who could think to say that *homo sapiens* is the only animal who could think to think."

10 FLEISSNER, ROBERT F. "Frost and Racism." *Negro American Literature Forum* 9 (Winter): 118-19.

Argues against those who have suggested that Frost was racist in his poetry or in his private dealings.

11 ____. "Frost and Tennyson: Factual as Well as 'Archetypal.'" *American Notes and Queries* 14 (December): 53-55.

Reminiscence of Frost at Bread Loaf, July 1960, and some Frost comments on Tennyson.

12 FOSTER, RICHARD. Review of *Frost: Centennial Essays*, edited by Jac Tharpe. *New England Quarterly* 48 (September): 455-58.

See 1974.83. Finds too much "stock academic stuff." The book as a whole, although it is attractively presented, is "a mighty disappointment."

13 FRENCH, ROBERTS W. "Reading Frost: 'The Road Not Taken.'" *English Record* (New York State English Council) 26 (Spring): 91-93.

"The speaker does *not* say that he took the road less travelled by; he says that he *will say*, in the distant future . . . that he took the road less travelled by." He will tell a lie.

14 HEATH, WILLIAM G., Jr. Review of *Robert Frost: A Pictorial Chronicle*, by Kathleen Morrison. *New England Quarterly* 48 (December): 590-92.

See 1974.61. "What one most derives from the words and photographs, however, is a sense, not of Frost's outward comings and goings, but of the inward qualities which underlay them."

15 HOEBER, DANIEL ROBERT. "The Many Marriages of Robert Frost: An Analysis of the Marriage Group in Frost's Poetry." *DAI* 36, 07A, p. 5298. Ph.D. dissertation, Southern Illinois University, 123 pp.

Concludes that "the marriage state in Frost's poetry is a major and hitherto unsuccessfully understood theme, the husband is at fault in any marriage conflict, and the poems of marital difficulty are veiled apologies to Elinor White Frost for problems he caused in their marriage."

16 HOLLAND, NORMAN N. "Unity Identity Text Self." *PMLA* 90 (October): 813-22.

Describes, in psychoanalytical terms, "identities governing levels of feedback." Frost uses his own themes and literary skills to make his poetry satisfying to himself. Compares Frost to Edwin Arlington Robinson to confirm the point. Reprinted: 1988.15.

17 HOUSE, ELIZABETH BALKMAN. "Robert Frost on Women and Marriage." *DAI* 36, 011A, p. 7422. Ph.D. dissertation, University of South Carolina, 179 pp.

Discusses Frost's language and metaphors for love and marriage. Sees marriage as a "stay against confusion."

18 KEMP, JOHN CROCKER. "Robert Frost Reconsidered: The Poet as Regionalist." *DAI* 36, 05A, p. 2823. Ph.D. dissertation, University of Pennsylvania, 323 pp.

Discusses Frost as a poet who was regional but transcends regionalism to achieve "great complexity and profound universality, and thus transcended the limitations inherent in his Yankee pose." Published as book: 1979.29.

19 KERN, ROBERT. "Toward a New Nature Poetry." *Centennial Review* 19 (Summer): 198-216.

Sees ways that twentieth-century nature poetry is very different from that of the nineteenth. Examines "Come In" as "a poem of 'stylistic crisis.'" Suggests that the poem causes a skepticism that makes the poet cautious about any similar situations in the future.

20 LENTRICCHIA, FRANK. *Robert Frost: Modern Poetics and the Landscapes of Self*. Durham, N.C.: Duke University Press, 200 pp.

Characterizes "the controlling urge of Frost's consciousness as a highly qualified and self-conscious urge to redeem, an urge to resolve tensions between self and the exterior, and to resolve tensions that reside wholly within the self."

21 LIBRARY OF CONGRESS. *Robert Frost: Lectures on the Centennial of His Birth*. Washington, D.C.: Library of Congress, 74 pp.

Reprints of 1974.2; 1974.22; 1975.27; and Tate, Allen, "'Inner Weather': Robert Frost as a Metaphysical Poet."

22 LIEBER, TODD M. "Robert Frost and Wallace Stevens: 'What to Make of a Diminished Thing.'" *American Literature* 47 (March): 64-83.

Finds parallels between the two poets, especially in their approach to "the metaphysical rather than the sociological dimensions of the waste land myth; for it was their inclination to view social conditions as the outgrowth of intellectual commitments."

23 McCLANAHAN, THOMAS HAYES. "Robert Frost: A Philosophical Perspective." *DAI* 30, 01A, p. 311. Ph.D. dissertation, University of South Carolina, 233 pp.

1975

Discusses the philosophical influences of Hume, William James, Henry James, Sr., and the American Puritans and transcendentalists on Frost's poetic thinking.

24 MARCUS, MORDECAI. "Motivation of Robert Frost's Hired Man." *College Literature* 3 (Winter): 63-68.

Analyzes the psychological motivation of Silas and his relationship to other characters in or named in the poem.

25 ____. "Robert Frost's 'Bond and Free': Structure and Meaning." *Concerning Poetry* 8 (Spring): 61-64.

Analyzes the themes in the poem. "The celebration of Love as opposed to the matter-of-factness about Thought suggests that Thought's distant discoveries and fusion are colder and more abstract than Love's unification of several beauty."

*26 OI, SOICHIRO. "Robert Frost no Shi ni tsuite" [Poetry of Robert Frost]. *Kansai Gaikokugo Daigaku Kenkyuronshu* (Japan) 22:109-28.

27 PACK, ROBERT. "Robert Frost's 'Enigmatic Reserve': The Poet as Teacher and Preacher." In *Robert Frost: Lectures on the Centennial of His Birth*. Washington, D.C.: Library of Congress, pp. 43-55.

Says Frost's "poems speak most profoundly when they speak by indirection; they are indeed 'dark sayings,' engagingly 'enigmatical,' and the best of them maintain Frost's characteristic 'reserve.'" Discusses "The Oven Bird," "The Most of It," "Acquainted with the Night," and "The Draft Horse." Reprinted: 1975.21.

28 PERRINE, LAURENCE. "The Tone of Frost's 'The Literate Farmer and the Planet Venus.'" *Notes on Contemporary Literature* 5 (May): 10-13.

Reply to 1974.73. Attempts to correct comments about the speaker's confusion in the poem.

29 POULE, LOIS ELAINE. "Robert Frost in the Posture of Simple Ignorance: A Study of Frost's Reading of Emerson's Poetry." *DAI* 36, 02A, p. 1975. Ph.D. dissertation, Indiana University, 164 pp.

Examines the poetry of Emerson and Frost and "the posture of their first-person speaker, derived from their common appreciation of what Emerson called 'simple ignorance.'"

30 POWELL, STEWART. "'Inspiration Is Hard to Find.'" *Washington Post*, 6 April, Section F, p. 11.

Relates the living arrangement of poet Edward Barna and his wife on Frost's former farm in Derry, New Hampshire, while awaiting delayed restoration of the farmhouse and land.

*31 SAWADA, SUKETARO. "Ralph Waldo Emerson to Robert Frost" [Ralph Waldo Emerson and Robert Frost]. *Gifu Joshi Daigaku Kiyo* (Japan) 4:123-38.

32 SEARS, JOHN F. "William James, Henri Bergson, and the Poetics of Robert Frost." *New England Quarterly* 48 (September): 341-61.

Discusses James's influence on Frost's ethics. "Bergson's impact was greatest on Frost's more mystical side, on his way of dealing with the mysteries of time, creation, and process."

33 SOKOL, BARNETT JEROME. "Robert Frost in England: His Poetry and Publications, 1912-1915." *DAI* 36, 05A, p. 2827. Ph.D. dissertation, Columbia University, 316 pp.

Discusses Frost's life and literary production while living in England. Sees Frost as having the opportunity "to reassess, and in some cases to discover, and confirm, his own American experiences and convictions."

34 SUTTON, WILLIAM A. "Robert Frost's Parents." *Ball State University Forum* 16 (Spring): 4-8.

Prints and comments on family materials made available by Lesley Frost Ballantine concerning her grandfather, William Prescott Frost, and grandmother, Belle Moodie Frost, during the San Francisco years.

*35 TAKIZAWA, YOICHI. "Robert Frost, 'A Masque of Reason' ni tsuite" [A study of Robert Frost's "A Masque of Reason"]. *Tsurumi Daigaku Kiyo Gaikokugo Hen* (Japan) 12:1-19.

36 UDALL, STEWART L. "Robert Frost, Kennedy, and Khrushchev: A Memoir of Poetry and Power." *Shenandoah* 26 (Winter): 52-68.

Describes his friendship with Frost during and after the Washington, D.C., years. Also recalls Frost's repeating the concluding lines from Sir John Davies' "The Immortality of the Soul," which he said "may be the best lines ever written by a poet."

37 VITELLI, JAMES R. Review of *Robert Frost: The Poet and His Critics*, by Donald J. Greiner. *New England Quarterly* 48 (December): 598-600.

See 1974.37. "Greiner has achieved a valuable critique of both Frost and us, his readers. His book should provide a major prodding to the revaluations of Frost now underway."

38 WIDDOWSON, H.G. *Stylistics and the Teaching of Literature*. London: Longman Group, pp. 104-7.

Examines "Dust of Snow" in terms of linguistic analysis.

39 WINSLOW, DONALD J. "The Origin of Frost's 'Witness Tree.'" *American Notes and Queries* 13 (June): 153-54.

Recounts the story of Frost's discovery of the "witness" tree as used by surveyors in former times to mark boundaries. Told by the son of Dr. Guy M. Winslow, president of Lasell Junior College (Auburndale, Mass.), who was acquainted with Frost and showed him an example of such a tree.

*40 YAMAKAWA, GAKUJI. "Frost no Shi niokeru Sekiryokan: 'Fuzai,' Vacancy no Ishiki ni tsuite" [Desolation in Frost's poems: Consciousness of absence and vacancy]. *Bunka Kiyo* (Hirosaki Daigaku Kyoyobu) (Japan) 9:89-96.

1976

*1 ANDO, CHIYOKO. "Robert Frost 'Shonen no Kokoro,' 1: Toguchi noaru Shi" [Robert Frost, "A Boy's Will," 1: A poem with a door]. *Saniku Gakuin Tankidaigaku Kiyo* (Japan) 5:77-104.

2 ANGYAL, ANDREW J., and KENT LJUNDQUIST. "Some Early Frost Imitations of Poe." *Poe Studies* 9 (June): 14-16.

Shows the influence of Poe on the juvenilia poems of Frost during his high school years in Lawrence, Mass.

3 APPLE, MAX. "The Oranging of America." In *The Oranging of America and Other Stories*. New York: Viking Penguin, pp. 3-19.

Short story satirizing the life of Howard Johnson, the hotel and restaurant tycoon. Includes an imaginary visit with Frost on his farm in New Hampshire in the 1930s. Frost is depicted as rustic, generous, and wise.

4 BARTINI, ARNOLD G. "Robert Frost and Moral Neutrality." *CEA Critic* 38 (January): 22-24.

Finds "an essential indifference to moral perspective," or neutrality regarding moral judgments in the poems.

5 BEACHAM, WALTON. "Technique and the Sense of Play in the Poetry of Robert Frost." In *Frost: Centennial Essays II*. Edited by Jac Tharpe. Jackson: University Press of Mississippi, pp. 246-61.

Considers Frost as a "playful" poet and analyzes how play is accomplished through language and poetic structure. Frost's use of irony is also explored.

6 BOOTH, PHILIP. "Frost's Empty Spaces." *Gone Into If Not Explained: Essays on Poems by Robert Frost*. Edited by Greg Kuzma. *Pebble* (Crete, Neb.), nos. 14-15, pp. 53-60.

Examines the desert metaphor. "Lonely as Frost is in the poem, and even more lonely as he will be, he is at least able to bare himself to, and to bear, whatever it is that is so unawares that it doesn't even account for him, or for his spirit. The poem knows it as Frost knew it. By the end of the poem he can admit to himself 'I have it in me. . . .' To scare himself. To write 'Desert Places.'"

7 BORROFF, MARIE. "Robert Frost: 'To Earthward.'" In *Frost: Centennial Essays II*. Edited by Jac Tharpe. Jackson: University Press of Mississippi, pp. 21-39.

A comparison-contrast of "To Earthward" and "Bond and Free," as both involve physical touch and exertion. Describes the labor-love analogy in Frost's poetry.

8 COOK, MARJORIE. "Acceptance in Frost's Poetry: Conflict as Play." In *Frost: Centennial Essays II*. Edited by Jac Tharpe. Jackson: University Press of Mississippi, pp. 223-35.

"What needs to be understood about Frost's acceptance, his comic vision, is that his affirmation includes the struggle. He does not choose between the dark and the bright. In a world in which the important successes are qualified, the question always is 'what to make of a diminished thing.'"

9 COXE, LOUIS O. "Frost's 'Spring Pools.'" *Gone Into If Not Explained: Essays on Poems by Robert Frost*. Edited by Greg Kuzma. *Pebble* (Crete, Neb.), nos. 14-15, pp. 155-59.

On the poem as a warning of "what can happen – what does happen – to a surplus in nature."

10 CUNNINGHAM, DONALD. "'Mending Wall.'" *Gone Into If Not Explained: Essays on the Poems of Robert Frost*. Edited by Greg Kuzma. *Pebble* (Crete, Neb.), nos. 14-15, pp. 65-73.

Suggests that the narrator of the poem is not necessarily the poet. "The poet asks us to 'go behind' the poem, and when we do, we see dramatically, rather than narratively, the inability of the poem's narrator to understand and communicate with the neighbor."

11 ECKE, JOANNA HEADSTREAM. "Fact as Dream: The Derry Love Poems of Robert Frost." *DAI* 37, 06A, pp. 3621-22. Ph.D. dissertation, Duke University, 227 pp.

Concludes that Frost implies Nature "is not sustaining, albeit that it offers hints of a greater spiritual reality. It is love and marriage which give an order to the world which can redeem the painful past and the confusing present."

12 EDWARDS, MARGARET. "The Play of 'Downward Comparisons': Animal Anthropomorphism in the Poems of Robert Frost." In *Frost: Centennial Essays II*. Edited by Jac Tharpe. Jackson: University Press of Mississippi, pp. 236-45.

Describes Frost's use of animals in the poems. "In almost all of Frost's poems that depict animals, anthropomorphism is a playful conceit used to lighten a dark tone, distract from strong feeling, and vivify realistic animal behavior."

13 FLEISSNER, ROBERT F. "Frost's and Yevtushenko's 'Irreverent Poems.'" *Notes on Contemporary Literature* 6 (January): 14-15.

Sees a parallel between Frost's "Forgive, O Lord" and Yevgeny Yevtushenko's "An Attempt at Blasphemy."

14 FORD, THOMAS W. "Invitations from a Thrush: Frost versus Whitman." *Walt Whitman Review* 22 (Spring): 166-67.

Suggests a parallel between Frost's thrush in "Come In" and Whitman's in "When Lilacs Last in the Dooryard Bloom'd."

15 FRENCH, WARREN. "Frost Country." In *Frost: Centennial Essays II*. Edited by Jac Tharpe. Jackson: University Press of Mississippi, pp. 5-20.

Compares Frost's reputation with earlier New England poets whose significance has faded–Whittier, Longfellow, James Russell Lowell, and others. Frost's "country" will last because he made it his own.

*16 FUJIMOTO, MASAKI. "Kodokuna Kogisha: Frost no Kojinshugi" [Lonely protester: Frost's individualism]. *Bungaku to Hyoron* (Japan) 12:54-64.

17 GAYLORD, ALAN T. "The Imaginary State of 'New Hampshire.'" In *Gone Into If Not Explained: Essays on the Poems of Robert Frost*. Edited by Greg Kuzma. *Pebble* (Crete, Neb.), nos. 14-15, pp. 5-52.

Describes the effect of the state of New Hampshire and the book of that title, and the significance of the effect on Frost's work as a whole.

18 GELPI, ALBERT. "Robert Frost: The Clearing in the Words." *Gone Into If Not Explained: Essays on the Poems of Robert Frost*. Edited by Greg Kuzma. *Pebble* (Crete, Neb.), nos. 14-15, pp. 111-26.

Examines Frost's purpose as that of the woodsman-pioneer in the American tradition.

19 GORDON, MARIE. "Robert Frost at Home." *Carrell* (University of Miami, Fla.), no. 17, pp. 9-12.

Provides a reminiscence of Frost in Ripton, Vt., and South Miami, by the mother of Phyllis Marie, the wife of William Prescott Frost III, grandson of Frost.

20 HALL, DOROTHY JUDD. "The Height of Feeling Free: Frost and Bergson." *Texas Quarterly* 19 (Spring): 128-43.

Suggests that in Bergson "Frost found a way to justify the Emersonian-Swedenborgian concept of an invisible universe in terms consistent with modern scientific theory – a means, also, of bringing into alignment Biblical metaphor and evolutionary hypotheses."

21 HALL, TED. "A Note on 'The Road Not Taken.'" *Gone Into If Not Explained: Essays on the Poems of Robert Frost*. Edited by Greg Kuzma. *Pebble* (Crete, Neb.), nos. 14-15, pp. 135-38.

On the irony of the poem and the "incongruity of present and future perspectives," though Frost is speaking tongue-in-cheek.

22 HARRIS, KATHRYN GIBBS. "Robert Frost and Science: The Shaping Metaphor of Motion in the Poems." *DAI* 37, 02A, p. 967. Ph.D. dissertation, Michigan State University, 234 pp.

Examines scientific and philosophical influences, especially those of William James, Henri Bergson, Emanuel Swedenborg, Albert Einstein, and Niels Bohr.

23 HART, JEFFREY. "Frost and Eliot." *Sewanee Review* 84 (July-September): 425-47.

Describes the relationship of the two poets and compares and contrasts their work. "Each complements the other. They are related dialectically, and the achievement of each is enhanced by that relationship."

24 HEARN, THOMAS K., Jr. "Making Sweetbreads Do: Robert Frost and Moral Empiricism." *New England Quarterly* 49 (March): 65-81.

Finds similarities in Frost to David Hume (1711-76). Refers to Frost's "Quandary." "Our moral awareness is grounded in our attitudes, feelings, or emotions rather than thought or reason. In moral decisions, we must, in the end, rely on, make do with, 'sweetbreads.'"

25 HUNTER, WILLIAM B., Jr. "An Evening with Robert Frost and Carl Sandburg." *Forum* (University of Houston) 13 (Winter): 51-55.

Recalls a Frost-Sandburg reading at Wofford College, South Carolina, in March 1950. Describes Frost's strong dislike for Sandburg and an inability "to tolerate anyone else who might share his adulation."

*26 ISHIDO, TETSUYA. "Robert Frost, 'A Masque of Reason' ni tsuite: Frost to Yobu" [Robert Frost's "A Masque of Reason": Frost and Job]. *Kochi Daigaku Gakujutsu Kenkyuhokoku, Jinbunkkagaku* (Japan) 25:123-30.

27 JONES, DEWITT. "Look of a Land Beloved." *National Geographic* 149 (April): 444-67.

A photographic portfolio, in color, of the New England landscapes and people, with well-chosen excerpts from the poetry.

*28 KANASEKI, TOSHIO. "Frost Girai: In New England There Lived a Poet" [Dislike of Frost: In New England there lived a poet]. *Eigo Bugaku Sekai* (Eicho-sha) (Japan) 10:2-6.

29 KAU, JOSEPH. "'Trust . . . to go by contraries': Incarnation and the Paradox of Belief in the Poetry of Frost." In *Frost: Centennial Essays II*. Edited by Jac Tharpe. Jackson: University Press of Mississippi, pp. 99-111.

Frost is not an agnostic, and he creates myths "which fix man's origins in the spiritual or divine, speak of his troubled existence, and hint at the possibility of return to the divine or spiritual." Frost believed that life is an act of faith, beginning in mystery and ending in hope: "the span between is paradox, to 'trust . . . to go by contraries' that are true."

30 KOCH, FREDERICK H., Jr. "Robert Frost at 75." *Carrell* (University of Miami, Fla.), no. 17, pp. 15-18.

Recalls Frost at the Winter Institute of Literature at the University of Miami and a production of "A Masque of Reason" to celebrate his seventy-fifth birthday.

31 KUMIN, MAXINE. "A Note on 'Provide, Provide.'" *Gone Into If Not Explained: Essays on the Poems of Robert Frost*. Edited by Greg Kuzma. *Pebble* (Crete, Neb.), nos. 14-15, pp. 61-64.

On the "hideously difficult-to-maintain rhyme scheme" of the poem.

32 KUZMA, GREG, ed. *Gone Into If Not Explained: Essays on Poems by Robert Frost*. *Pebble* (Crete, Neb.), nos. 14-15. , 173 pp.

Contents: Alan T. Gaylord, "The Imaginary State of 'New Hampshire'"; Philip Booth, "Frost's Empty Spaces"; Maxine Kumin, "A Note on 'Provide, Provide'"; Donald Cunningham, "'Mending Wall'"; William Meredith, "A Fratricide: Robert Frost's 'The Vanishing Red'"; Robert Narveson, "'Two Tramps in Mud Time': Thoreau versus 'Poor Richard'"; Linda Ray Pratt, "Prosody as Meaning in Frost's 'The Hill Wife'"; Albert Gelpi, "Robert Frost: The Clearing in the Words"; William H. Pritchard, "Bearing Witness: 'The Wind and the Rain'"; Ted Hall, "A Note on 'The Road Not Taken'"; Richard Wilbur, "On Robert Frost's 'The Gum-Gatherer'"; Roy Scheele, "The Laborious Dream: Frost's 'After Apple-Picking'"; Louis O. Coxe, "Frost's 'Spring Pools'"; John F. Lynen, "'I Will Sing You One-O.'"

33 LENTRICCHIA, FRANK, and MELISSA CHRISTENSEN LENTRICCHIA, comps. *Robert Frost: A Bibliography, 1913-1974*. Scarecrow Author Bibliographies, no. 25. Metuchen, N.J.: Scarecrow Press, 238 pp.

Provides, without annotations, lists of primary and secondary Frost material, plus a "bibliographical history" of specific poems.

34 LYNEN, JOHN F. "'I Will Sing You One-O.'" *Gone Into If Not Explained: Essays on the Poems of Robert Frost*. Edited by Greg Kuzma. *Pebble* (Crete, Neb.), nos. 14-15, pp. 161-70.

Interprets the possibilities of "'one o'clock,' 'a single zero,' or 'one, oh! (alas).'" Finds possibilities for symbolic meanings.

35 McCLANAHAN, THOMAS. "Frost's Theodicy: 'Word I Had No One Left but God.'" In *Frost: Centennial Essays II*. Edited by Jac Tharpe. Jackson: University Press of Mississippi, pp. 112-26.

Frost's intellectual preoccupations are parallel to those of William James. Thus he is skeptical about traditional religious concerns. "Ultimately, Frost's theodicy revolves around the recognition of both human and divine finitude."

36 MacLEISH, ARCHIBALD. "Robert Frost and New England." *National Geographic* 149 (April): 439-44.

Introduces color photographs (pp. 444-67) of New England scenes by Dewitt Jones. Describes Frost as a New Englander and shows how he uses the New England setting to reveal "ourselves: our condition as men: our consciousness as human beings."

37 MARCUS, MORDECAI. "Motivation of Frost's Hired Man." *College Literature* 3 (Winter): 63-68.

Sees the couple, Mary and Warren, as detached mother and father to Silas and their farm as home to him.

38 ____. "The Whole Pattern of Robert Frost's 'Two Witches': Contrasting Psychosexual Modes." *Literature and Psychology* 26, no. 2:69-78.

Discusses "The Pauper Witch of Grafton" and "The Witch of Coös" in terms of psychodynamic analysis.

39 MASON, JULIAN. "Frost's Conscious Accommodation of Contraries." *CEA Critic* 38 (March): 26-31.

Describes Frost's ways to bring "opposites together in some type of usually dramatic context which makes both character and reader aware not only of the existence of each of the two facets, but more importantly, of their opposing aspects as well."

40 MATTHEWS, MARJORIE SWANK. "Issues and Answers in the Book of Job and Joban Issues and Answers in Three Twentieth Century Writers: Carl Jung, Robert Frost, and Archibald MacLeish." *DAI* 37, 012A, p. 7800. Ph.D. dissertation, Florida State University, 153 pp.

Examines the Book of Job as it appears in the Hebrew canon and sees two major issues: the doctrine of divine retribution and the meaning of life. Discusses "A Masque of Reason" in this context.

41 MAYNARD, JOYCE. "Robert Frost Gets His Road and His Day in Vermont." *New York Times*, 30 August, Section 3, p. 25.

Nearly 100 attended a ceremony in Green Mountain National Forest opening a memorial nature trail on Robert Frost Day.

42 MEREDITH, WILLIAM. "A Fratricide: Robert Frost's 'The Vanishing Red.'" *Gone Into If Not Explained: Essays on the Poems of Robert Frost*. Edited by Greg Kuzma. *Pebble* (Crete, Neb.), nos. 14-15, pp. 75-80.

Examines the poem, which "addresses itself to a perennial mystery which it wants to put before us, without historical cause: an irrational race prejudice, strong enough to do murder." Also analyzes the poem metrically.

43 MILLER, DAVID. L. "Dominion of the Eye in Frost." In *Frost: Centennial Essays II*. Edited by Jac Tharpe. Jackson: University Press of Mississippi, pp. 141-58.

On Frost's "seeing" and his visual imagination. Contrasts Frost and the English Romantics and Milton. "When he does approach the theme of subjective autonomy over sense experience, he approaches it entirely by way of the eye, manipulating ordinary perception to create a playful illusion of visionary power."

44 MONTEIRO, GEORGE. "Frost's Quest for the 'Purple-Fringed.'" *English Language Notes* 13 (March): 204-6.

Describes Frost's confusion of "orchis" with "gentian" before he became familiar with the wild flowers of New England.

45 MONTGOMERY, MARION. "Robert Frost: One Who Shrewdly Pretends." In *Frost: Centennial Essays II*. Edited by Jac Tharpe. Jackson: University Press of Mississippi, pp. 213-22.

Frost is "a wily Odysseus, one who believes that in the interest of survival in strange seas it pays to be shifty and secretive." Frost often "is playing a private game in his poetry, a poetry disguised as public through its particulars."

46 MORSE, STEARNS. "'The Subverted Flower': An Exercise in Triangulation." In *Frost: Centennial Essays II*. Edited by Jac Tharpe. Jackson: University Press of Mississippi, pp. 170-76.

Discusses the poem as "unFrostian" because it deals openly with sex. The meaning may be explained by its placement with other poems in *A Witness Tree*.

47 NARVESON, ROBERT. "'Two Tramps in Mud Time': Thoreau versus 'Poor Richard.'" *Gone Into If Not Explained: Essays on the Poems of Robert Frost*. Edited by Greg Kuzma. *Pebble* (Crete, Neb.), nos. 14-15, pp. 81-94.

On Frost's narrative method and the reconciliation of the New-England work-ethic with Thoreau's idea of "self-satisfying work."

48 NITCHIE, GEORGE W. "Robert Frost: Some Reflections on Poetry and Power." In *Frost: Centennial Essays II*. Edited by Jac Tharpe. Jackson: University Press of Mississippi, pp. 40-47.

On Frost's brush with power in the John F. Kennedy administration. Unlike Yeats, he was not an official "smiling public man," although the recognition did eventually come from the Congress and the president.

49 PERKINS, DAVID. "Robert Frost." In *A History of Modern Poetry: From the 1890s to the High Modernist Mode*. Cambridge, Mass.: Harvard University Press, pp. 227-51.

Finds Frost "modern" in that he "belongs essentially to the Romantic tradition, but as a critique. He invokes Romantic convention in order to correct it." Also: "Frost's poetic idiom is a unified achievement on three lines, all deliberately pursued. It is colloquially simple; it is dramatic, and it is racy of a locality, a region."

50 PERRINE, LAURENCE. "Frost's 'I Will Sing You One-O.'" *Explicator* 34 (February): Item 48.

Suggests possible meanings for "one-o," including reference to the folk song "Green Grow the Rushes-O."

51 ____. "Robert Frost and the Idea of Immortality." In *Frost: Centennial Essays II*. Edited by Jac Tharpe. Jackson: University Press of Mississippi, pp. 85-98.

Shows that Frost "found value both in uncertainty about a future life and in faith in it; that his own poetry is nevertheless earth-centered, not heaven-centered; and that he increasingly leaned toward a conviction that the soul would continue to exist after death, not disembodied in some other world, but reembodied upon earth."

52 PRATT, LINDA RAY. "Prosody as Meaning in Frost's 'The Hill Wife.'" *Gone Into If Not Explained: Essays on the Poems of Robert Frost*. Edited by Greg Kuzma. *Pebble* (Crete, Neb.), nos. 14-15, pp. 95-109.

Analyzes the poem as a "*tour de force* of Frost's ability to combine and modify the traditions of the lyric, the narrative, and the dramatic monologue in a series of 'spoken' poems in which rhyme and meter control meaning through their control of sound." Analyzes the scansion of sections of the poem.

53 PRITCHARD, WILLIAM H. "Bearing Witness: 'The Wind and the Rain.'" *Gone Into If Not Explained: Essays on the Poems of Robert Frost*. Edited by Greg Kuzma. *Pebble* (Crete, Neb.), nos. 14-15, pp. 127-34.

Discusses "Frost's best unknown poem," which is probably his "most immediate artistic response" to his wife's death.

54 ____. "The Grip of Frost." *Hudson Review* 29 (Summer): 185-204.

Describes early examples of Frost's "sound and sense" and the poetic voice, while residing in England.

55 PROFITT, EDWARD. "Frost's Journey from Gloom." *Research Studies* (Washington State University) 44 (December): 248-51.

Finds Frost "most of all asks to be read against the latter nineteenth century," because of his theme of "the journey from gloom" recurrent in the poetry.

*56 RAABE, DAVID MARLIN. "Computerized Scansion of the Poetry of Robert Frost." Ph.D. dissertation, University of Nebraska, 224 pp.

57 REED, RICHARD. "The Animal World in Robert Frost's Poetry." In *Frost: Centennial Essays II*. Edited by Jac Tharpe. Jackson: University Press of Mississippi, pp. 159-69.

Frost's use of animals in the poetry changes dramatically from the romantic confidence in nature in *A Boy's Will* to a realistic, unsentimental view in later works, proclaiming "human superiority."

58 ROOD, KAREN LANE. "Robert Frost's 'Sentence Sounds': Wildness Opposing the Sonnet Form." In *Frost: Centennial Essays II*. Edited by Jac Tharpe. Jackson: University Press of Mississippi, pp. 196-210.

Frost is able to control "wildness" in his sonnets, the best ones being those "in which the wildness of the sentence sounds is strong." Thus "Design" is superior to "Why Wait for Science?"

59 No entry.

60 ROSNER, GEORGE W. "Robert Frost at the University of Miami." *Carrell* (University of Miami, Fla.), no. 17, pp. 12-15.

Provides a reminiscence of the Frosts in Key West in 1934-35 and his friendship with Hervey Allen, author of *Anthony Adverse*.

1976

61 SANDERS, DAVID ALAN. "Revelation as Child's Play in Frost's 'Directive.'" In *Frost: Centennial Essays II*. Edited by Jac Tharpe. Jackson: University Press of Mississippi, pp. 267-77.

A close analysis of the poem, focusing on the reader's and the poet's participation in it. "As the metaphor of the Eucharist implies, both we and the speaker are necessary to give this body life. Only if we see does his imagination live; if we cannot identify with him, he is dead. As our salvation depends on him, so his survival depends on us."

*62 SAWADA, SUKETARO. "Esuman ni Taisura no Response: Kotei to Hitei" [Frost's response to Emerson: Affirmation and negation]. *Nanzan Eibugaku* (Nanzan Daigaku Daigakuin) (Japan) 1:46-61.

63 SCHEELE, ROY. "The Laborious Dream: Frost's 'After Apple-Picking.'" *Gone Into If Not Explained: Essays on the Poems of Robert Frost*. Edited by Greg Kuzma. *Pebble* (Crete, Neb.), nos. 14-15, pp. 145-53.

On the significance of the dream idea in the poem. "The dream that recalls the harvest is a prelude to the deeper dreaming of sleep, to a further redefinition of experience, and it is the measure of this human sleep that the harvest must go on."

64 SOKOL, B.J. "What Went Wrong Between Robert Frost and Ezra Pound." *New England Quarterly* 49 (December): 521-41.

Suggests that Frost rejected imagism, but felt rejected himself; his value as a poet seemed to be ignored, contributing to an overwhelming lack of self-confidence.

65 STANLIS, PETER J. Review of *Robert Frost: Modern Poetics and the Landscape of Self* by Frank Lentricchia. *New England Quarterly* 49 (June): 320-22.

See 1975.20. "This book is the best conceived, best structured, best written, the most profound critical study of Frost's poetry since John Lynen's *The Pastoral Art of Robert Frost* (1960) and Reuben Brower's *The Poetry of Robert Frost* (1963)."

66 ____. "Robert Frost: Politics in Theory and Practice." In *Frost: Centennial Essays II*. Edited by Jac Tharpe. Jackson: University Press of Mississippi, pp. 48-82.

As an individualist, Frost has reservations about political sides, especially extreme ones. Also, "Frost's tragic vision of life was reinforced by his conviction that even within the temporal order the power of politics was severely restricted by limitations within human nature."

67 SUTTON, WILLIAM A., ed. *Newdick's Season of Frost: An Interrupted Biography of Robert Frost*. Introduction by Lesley Frost. Albany, N.Y.: State University of New York Press, 454 pp.

Prints Newdick's incomplete manuscript of a biography of Frost. Also includes research notes.

68 TAYLOR, ANYA. "A Frost Debt to Beddoes." *English Language Notes* 13 (June): 291-92.

Compares Frost's "Stopping by Woods on a Snowy Evening" to Thomas Lovell Beddoes' "The Phantom Wooer" in terms of diction and theme.

69 THARPE, JAC [L.], ed. *Frost: Centennial Essays II*. Jackson: University Press of Mississippi, 322 pp.

Contents: J[ac] T[harpe], "Frost Country"; Warren French, "Frost Country"; Marie Borroff, "Robert Frost: 'To Earthward'"; George W. Nitchie, "Robert Frost: Some Reflections on Poetry and Power"; Peter J. Stanlis, "Robert Frost: Politics in Theory and Practice"; J[ac] T[harpe], "Religion"; Laurence Perrine, "Robert Frost and the Idea of Immortality"; Joseph Kau, "'Trust . . . to Go by Contraries': Incarnation and the Paradox of Belief in the Poetry of Frost"; Thomas McClanahan, "Frost's Theodicy: 'Word I Had No One Left but God'"; J[ac] T[harpe], "Method and Theory"; David M. Wyatt, "Choosing in Frost"; David L. Miller, "Dominion of the Eye in Frost"; Richard Reed, "The Animal World in Frost's Poetry"; Stearns Morse, "'The Subverted Flower': An Exercise in Triangulation"; Patricia Wallace, "The 'Estranged Point of View': The Thematics of Imagination in Frost's Poetry"; Karen Lane Rood, "Robert Frost's 'Sentence Sounds': Wildness Opposing the Sonnet Form"; J[ac] T[harpe], "Play"; Marion Montgomery, "Robert Frost: One Who Shrewdly Pretends"; Marjorie Cook, "Acceptance in Frost's Poetry: Conflict as Play"; Margaret Edwards, "The Play of 'Downward Comparisons': Animal Anthropomorphism in the Poems of Robert Frost"; Walton Beacham, "Technique and the Sense of Play in the Poetry of Robert Frost"; Stephen D. Warner, "The Control of Play and the Play of Control in Robert Frost's Poetry"; David Alan Sanders, "Revelation as Child's Play in Frost's 'Directive'"; J[ac] T[harpe], "Background and Biography"; Thomas Daniel Young, "Our Two Worthies: Robert Frost and John Crowe Ransom"; Perry Westbrook, "Abandonment and

Desertion in the Poetry of Robert Frost"; Dorothy Tyler, "The Strong Are Saying Nothing."

70 THOMPSON, LAWRANCE, and R.H. WINNICK. *Robert Frost: Later Years, 1938-1963.* New York: Holt, Rinehart and Winston, 468 pp.

Third volume of the authorized biography begun in 1939, completed by Winnick after Thompson's illness and incapacitation in 1972. Describes Frost's activities following the death of Elinor Frost and publication of the masques, books of poetry, and individual poems until Frost's death on 29 January 1963.

71 TWOMBLY, ROBERT G. "The Poetics of Demur: Lowell and Frost." *College English* 38 (December): 373-92.

Finds in Robert Lowell and Frost that "the most compelling gesture of obligation is the final demur, the turning away into silence. Time after time the implicit subject of their poetry is contact or the failure of contact, love or its transmutation into aggression or malice."

72 TYLER, DOROTHY. "The Strong Are Saying Nothing." In *Frost: Centennial Essays II.* Edited by Jac Tharpe. Jackson: University Press of Mississippi, pp. 305-16.

An account, by an admirer, of the death and burial of Frost and matters concerning the Frost family and estate.

73 VAIL, DENNIS. "Robert Frost's Imagery and the Poetic Consciousness." *Graduate Studies: Texas Tech University*, no. 12 (March): 83.

Describes "the *way* Frost's lyric imagery works," especially that of trees and woods. The imagery "suggests, if only among other things, the private poetic world and what happens there."

74 WALLACE, PATRICIA BOYLE. "The 'Estranged Point of View': The Thematics of Imagination in Frost's Poetry." In *Frost: Centennial Essays II.* Edited by Jac Tharpe. Jackson: University Press of Mississippi, pp. 177-95.

On women as "outsiders" in Frost's poetry. They are "'allegorical' figures for the imagination." Discusses "the Hill Wife," the "witch" poems, and "Paul's Wife."

75 ____. "Recognition and Surprise: The Poet's Voice in the Poems of Robert Frost." *DAI* 37, 08A, p. 5132. Ph.D. dissertation, University of Iowa, 195 pp.

Examines Frost's poetry as acts of speaking and listening. Sees Frost as attempting "to discover a fully individual poetic voice through which to overcome confinement."

76 WARNER, STEPHEN D. "The Control of Play and the Play of Control in Robert Frost's Poetry." In *Frost: Centennial Essays II*. Edited by Jac Tharpe. Jackson: University Press of Mississippi, pp. 262-66.

Frost's playfulness is part of his metaphorical method in the poetry. "The importance of the sense of play is to provide respite from and insight into reality."

77 WATERS, GREGORY. "'Directive': Frost's Magical Mystery Tour." *Concerning Poetry* 9 (Spring): 33-38.

"'Directive' is a poetic tour de force, an accomplishment that goes further than all of Frost's poetry, both in terms of its craftsmanship and its diabolical intent. We are in his power from the start, and respond blindly to his words just as he directs."

78 WESTBROOK, PERRY. "Abandonment and Desertion in the Poetry of Robert Frost." In *Frost: Centennial Essays II*. Edited by Jac Tharpe. Jackson: University Press of Mississippi, pp. 291-304.

On sentimentality in the poetry. Through irony, Frost neutralizes what otherwise might be merely sentimental.

79 WILBUR, RICHARD. *Gone Into If Not Explained: Essays on the Poems of Robert Frost*. Edited by Greg Kuzma. *Pebble* (Crete, Neb.), nos. 14-15, pp. 138-43.

Sees the gum-gatherer as "a poet who has ascended some distance above the daily flux so as to distil it into something of the first water."

80 WYATT, DAVID M. "Choosing in Frost." In *Frost: Centennial Essays II*. Edited by Jac Tharpe. Jackson: University Press of Mississippi, pp. 129-40.

Although Frost often writes about choices, as in "The Road Not Taken," there is much more involved in the act of choosing. "Through this very self-conscious performance he reveals the prevailing mode of his poetry: Frost does not choose form so much as find himself chosen by it. The surprise of the writer becomes the surprise of the reader."

1976

81 YOUNG, THOMAS DANIEL. "Our Two Worthies: Robert Frost and John Crowe Ransom." In *Frost: Centennial Essays II*. Edited by Jac Tharpe. Jackson: University Press of Mississippi, pp. 281-90.

On the literary friendship of the two poets, beginning in 1918. As a reader for Holt, Frost recommended publication of Ransom's first book, *Poems About God*. Describes several occasions the two poets were together. Frost said in 1956 at Kenyon College, "You have right here on this campus the greatest living American poet."

1977

1 BACON, HELEN. "For Girls: From 'Birches' to 'Wild Grapes.'" *Yale Review* 67 (Autumn): 13-29.

Analyzes "Wild Grapes" as a poem for girls, written at the urging of Susan Hayes Ward, as a companion piece to "Birches," which she read as a poem for boys.

2 BIEGANOWSKI, RONALD. "Realms of the Spirit: An Inquiry into Robert Frost's Sense of Place." *DAI* 38, 04A, p. 2119. Ph.D. dissertation, Fordham University, 208 pp.

Examines the books of poetry chronologically and concludes: "A continuous story of search, discovery and growth emerges from a tracing of Frost's religious consciousness through his books of poetry," springing from his sense of place.

3 BROMWICH, DAVID. "The Bleakest of Lords." *New York Times Book Review*, 16 January, pp. 4-5, 28.

Review of 1976.67 and 1976.70. Finds Frost essentially "mean and desperate" in his later years.

4 BROYARD, ANATOLE. "Books of the Times." *New York Times*, 19 January, Section C, p. 20.

Review of 1976.70. Notes that Frost was "a remarkably petty and selfish man."

5 CRANE, JOAN St.C. "Robert Frost's 'Kitty Hawk.'" *Studies in Bibliography*, no. 30, pp. 241-49.

Describes the bibliographical history and the themes of the poem. Includes a textual collation of all versions.

6 D'AVANZO, MARIO L. "Frost's 'Departmental' and Emerson: A Further Range of Satire." *Concerning Poetry* 10 (Fall): 67-69.

Finds Frost's source for the ant in Emerson's "Nature," as well as in Proverbs.

7 ____. "How to Build a Chimney: Frost Gleans Thoreau." *Thoreau Journal Quarterly* 9 (October): 24-26.

Suggests chapter 13 of *Walden*, "House-Warming," and Thoreau's description of building his brick chimney as the source for Frost's "The Kitchen Chimney."

8 DURDEN, FRED. "Thoreau and Frost: Birds of a Feather." *Thoreau Journal Quarterly* 9 (October): 28-32.

On the influence of Thoreau's loon passage in *Walden* on Frost's "The Oven Bird."

9 FLEISSNER, ROBERT F. Review of *Newdick's Season of Frost: An Interrupted Biography of Robert Frost*, edited by William A. Sutton. *New England Quarterly* 50 (June): 351-53.

See 1976.67. Finds numerous editorial errors in mechanics and facts, along with glaring printing mistakes.

10 ____. "Stopping Yet Again by Frost's Woods." *Research Studies* (Washington State University) 45 (March): 45-49.

Examines the various symbolic interpretations of the poem and offers a Jungian perspective.

11 GREINER, DONALD J. "The Biography of Robert Frost: An Essay Review." *Resources for American Literary Study* 7 (Autumn): 162-76.

Surveys the biographies of Frost and concludes that Thompson's study (1976.70) is "an impressive achievement" characterized by "impeccable scholarship."

12 HENDERSON, ARCHIBALD. "Robert Frost's 'Out, Out–.'" *American Imago* 34 (Spring): 12-27.

Interprets the poem in terms of Freudian theories of sexual symbols and "a series of socio-sexual crises."

13 HENRY, NAT. "Frost's 'Acquainted with the Night.'" *Explicator* 35 (Spring): 28-29.

Reply to Martin (vol. 26, item 64). Attempts to clarify the tone of the poem.

*14 HIGASHIYAMA, MASAYOSHI. "Kataru Frost" [Frost talks]. *Ashiya Daigaku Ronso* (Japan) 2:49-62.

1977

15 KAU, JOSEPH. "Frost's 'A Concept Self-Conceived.'" *Explicator* 35 (Spring): 19.

The poem implies that "belief is valuable, that it should be perpetuated, and perhaps that it is essential."

16 ____. "Two Notes on Robert Frost Poems: Frost's 'Version' of Zeno's Arrow" and "Blind Optimism in Frost's 'We Vainly Wrestle.'" *Notes on Modern American Literature* 1 (Fall): Item 33.

Suggests in the first note that "Frost through his parody of Zeno's paradox implies that the attempt at affirming non-existence of spirit that is eternal, symbolized by the myth of the Phoenix, is as absurd as Zeno's attempt to argue non-movement in a moving arrow." Note two is on Frost's "belief as opposed to unbelief, existence as opposed to non-existence."

17 LEHMAN-HAUPT, CHRISTOPHER. "Books of the Times." *New York Times*, 5 October, Section C, p. 23.

Review of *Robert Frost: The Work of Knowing*, by Richard Poirier (1977.30):"With its complex and brilliantly subtle readings ... it provokes us to start over again with Frost."

18 LISCHER, TRACY KENYON. "The Passive Voice in American Literature: Vehicle for Tragedy in [William Hill] Brown, Hawthorne, O'Neill, Wharton, and Frost." *DAI* 39, 03A, p. 1573. Ph.D. dissertation, St. Louis University, 179 pp.

Discusses "Directive" as illustrating "a functioning dualist philosophy and the concept of reality as a process of ever-shifting tensions between opposites."

19 MELVIN, BETSY, and TOM MELVIN. *Robert Frost Country*. Foreword by William Meredith. Garden City, N.Y.: Doubleday & Co., [124 pp.].

Original color photographs, some black-and-white, with excerpts from the poems. Meredith draws attention to images in "Hyla Brook."

20 MONTEIRO, GEORGE. "Emily Dickinson and Robert Frost." *Prairie Schooner* 51 (Winter): 369-86.

Finds some poetic antecedents of Frost poems in some of Dickinson's. Describes the coincidence of residency for both in Amherst, Mass.

21 MOORE, ANDY J. "Frost – and Lowell – at Midnight." *Southern Quarterly* 15 (April): 291-95.

Analyzes Robert Lowell's poem, "Robert Frost," published in 1969.

22 MULLINS, JOHN J. "Another Poet in the Frost House." *Washington Post*, 30 May, Section D, p. 7.

Announces that poet Katha Pollitt will begin her term as poet-in-residence in Franconia, N.H., and will live in the Frost house.

*23 NARITA, MICHIKO. "'Boston no Kita' no Eclogue: Frost no Keikentekijiga" [Eclogue of *North of Boston*: Frost's empirical ego]. *Jissen Eibungaku* (Japan) 11:52-72.

*24 OI, SOICHIRO. "Robert Frost no Shinshofukei" [Imagery landscape of Robert Frost]. *Kansai Gaikokugo Daigaku Kenkyuronshu* (Japan) 25:205-42.

*25 OKA, JUKICHI. "Robert Frost to Edward Thomas" [Robert Frost and Edward Thomas]. *Eigaku Ronko* (Tokyo Gakugei Daigaku) 9:4-11.

*26 ONJOHJI, YASUKO. "Frost no Gekishi no Nijuishikikozo" [The double structure of consciousness in Frost's dramatic poems]. *Tokyo Yakka Daigaku Ippankyoiku Kenkyukiyo* 4:1-7.

27 PERRINE, LAURENCE. "Frost's 'West-Running Brook,' 1-4, 16-29." *Explicator* 35 (Summer): 26-27.

Sees the two passages as parallel, representing the voice of the poet himself as the narrator.

28 ____. "A Set of Notes for Frost's Two Masques." *Resources for American Literary Study* 7 (Autumn): 125-33.

Provides annotations for footnotes clarifying allusions and references in the masques.

29 ____. "Teaching Ambiguity: Some Roads Not to Be Taken." *English in Texas* 8 (Summer): 78-80.

Rebuts Pollock (1977.32). Sees only ambiguities that add to the meaning of the poem. Rejects ingenious ambiguity-hunting that cancels out meaning.

30 POIRIER, RICHARD. *Robert Frost: The Work of Knowing*. New York: Oxford University Press, 322 pp.

Provides a critical exploration of the complexities of Frost's poetry and how the reader must "work" to "know" the implications of supposedly simple poems. Finds influence of Ralph Waldo Emerson. Suggests that there are sexual overtones in several poems. Reissued: 1990.15.

31 ____. "Soundings for Home: Frost's Poetry of Extravagance and Return." *Georgia Review* 31 (Summer): 286-315.

Sees Frost as "a poet who finds his freedom of movement out of a sense of restraint: the movement to one extreme is provoked by the imminence of the other."

32 POLLOCK, JOHN J. "On Robert Frost's 'The Road Not Taken.'" *English in Texas* 8 (Winter): 28-29.

Contends that the speaker in the poem took the *more* traveled road. Finds ambiguities in the poem to illustrate many ways to interpret poetry.

33 ROOKE, CONSTANCE. "The Elusive/Allusive Voice: An Interpretation of Frost's 'A Servant to Servants.'" *Cimarron Review* 38 (January): 13-23.

Discusses the presence of Frost in the poems as "*essentially* elusive."

*34 SAWADA, SUKETARO. "Robert Frost Niokeru Jitsuzonshugi" [Existentialism in Robert Frost]. *Bungaku to Hyoron* (Bugakuto Hyoron Sha] (Japan) 8:48-54.

*35 ____. "Tonooka Tatsuo to Robert Frost: Jitsuzontetsugakuteki Siten Karano Ichikosatsu" [Tatsuo Tonooka and Robert Frost: An existentialist study]. *Gifu Joshi Daigaku Kiyo* (Japan) 6:135-46.

36 SCHEELE, ROY. "Sensible Confusion in Frost's 'The Subverted Flower.'" *South Carolina Review* 10 (November): 89-98.

"Frost here seems to disappear in the poem's stylistic details much in the manner of the anonymous balladeer. The result is a freedom of narrative perspective which gives the impression of impartiality while at the same time providing a means of judging the actions of the boy and girl in the poem."

37 SEARS, JOHN F. Review of *Frost: Centennial Essays II*, edited by Jac Tharpe. *New England Quarterly* 50 (September): 531-33.

See 1976.69. Finds the collection very uneven, illustrating "a set of ideas Frost is presumed to have about the world without making judgments about how well the particular poems work."

38 SOKOL, B.J. "The Publication of Robert Frost's First Books: Triumph and Fiasco." *Book Collector* 26 (Summer): 228-39.

Details events in Frost's relationship with the David Nutt publishing company and Mrs. Alfred Nutt, widow of the son of the firm's founder. The story is "a sad and curious one, in which quixotic business practices, difficult personalities and anger turned a generous risk into loss and defeat."

39 SPENCER, BENJAMIN T. Review of *Robert Frost: Later Years, 1938-1963*, by Lawrance Thompson and R.H. Winnick. *American Literature* 49 (November): 447-49.

See 1976.70. Finds the approach more balanced in this volume as opposed to the previous ones. This last one does "convincingly mingle 'sympathy with critical detachment.'"

40 WAGNER, LINDA W. *Robert Frost: The Critical Reception*. New York: B. Franklin, 280 pp.

Reprints representative reviews of Frost's books in order of appearance.

41 WOLFE, GEOFFREY. "The Dark Side of Frost." *Washington Post*, 20 March, Section H, pp. 1, 4.

Review of *Robert Frost: Later Years, 1938-1963*, by Lawrance Thompson and R.H. Winnick (1976.70). Suggests that the public and private Frosts are difficult to accept, but finds Thompson's work overall to be monumental.

42 WOOD, SUSAN. "One Man's Frost." *Washington Post*, December 18, Section E, p. 3.

Review of *Robert Frost: The Work of Knowing*, by Richard Poirier (1977.30). Finds the book "not for the casual reader." Says most contemporary criticism is "too dense," yet pronounces Poirier "brilliant."

1978

1 ABEL, DARREL. "Robert Frost's 'True Make-Believe.'" *Texas Studies in Language and Literature* 20 (Winter): 552-78.

On Frost's beliefs as stated in his "Education by Poetry. . . ." Includes a new interpretation and solution to the mystery of Frost's poem, "Maple."

2 ANGYAL, ANDREW J. "Robert Frost's Poetry Before 1913: A Checklist." In *Proof, 5: The Yearbook of American Bibliographical and Textual Studies*. Edited by Joseph Katz. Columbia, S.C.: J. Faust & Co., pp. 67-125.

"This checklist is an attempt at putting the record in order. It has four major sections." The first records poems written before *A Boy's Will*. The second deals with poems with unresolved problems of attribution or date. The third is a group of appendices pertinent to attribution and dating. Fourth, is an index to the preceding three sections.

3 BACON, HELEN. "Dialogue of Poets: *Mens Animi* and the Renewal of Words." *Massachusetts Review* 19 (Summer): 319-34.

On Frost and the classical poets, especially Catullus and Ovid, and what he called "the renewal of words, . . . the making of words to mean again what they meant." (Delivered as the Elizabeth Drew Memorial Lecture at the Bread Loaf School of English, Bread Loaf, Vt., 12 July 1977.)

4 BANNOW, STEVEN WALKER. "Order and Arrangement in Robert Frost's Books of Poetry." *DAI* 39, 10A, p. 6125. Ph.D. dissertation, University of South Carolina, 528 pp.

Examines the books in detail chronologically to analyze Frost's poetic development.

5 BERRY, LINDA POTTER. "Sexual Development in the Poetry of Robert Frost." *DAI* 39, 12A, p. 7344. Ph.D. dissertation, University of South Carolina, 327 pp.

Argues that Frost does "devote a large portion of his work to a complete and relatively modern analysis of human sexual development. Discusses the various stages of sexual discovery from childhood to maturity and expressions of it in the poetry.

6 BLEAU, N. ARTHUR. "Robert Frost's Favorite Poem." With a Note by Lesley Frost. In *Frost: Centennial Essays III*. Edited by Jac Tharpe. Jackson: University Press of Mississippi, pp. 174-77.

Bleau relates the real circumstances behind "Stopping by Woods. . . ." Unable to sell some farm goods in town, Frost returned home knowing he would not be able to provide the necessary things for his family's Christmas. Just north of his farm, his horse (Eunice) stopped, and Frost "bawled like a baby." The details of the story are corroborated by his daughter, as he had privately told her.

7 CLARK, WALTER H., Jr. "The Work of Knowing Frost." *Michigan Quarterly Review* 17 (Summer): 392-403.

Review article on 1976.32, 1976.67, 1976.70, 1977.30. Describes the essential contribution of each work.

8 COOK, REGINALD L. "Robert Frost in Context." In *Frost: Centennial Essays III*. Edited by Jac Tharpe. Jackson: University Press of Mississippi, pp. 123-73.

"This essay covers a period of forty years. It taps the resources of Frost's private conversations as well as his public statements. Secondly, it establishes their context. Thirdly, wherever appropriate, it relates them to his poetry. And lastly, it documents them." Stresses the necessity to quote Frost in context and not to misrepresent what he said in person and in the poetry.

9 DOMINA, LYLE. "Thoreau and Frost: The Search for Reality." *Ball State University Forum* 19 (Autumn): 67-72.

Sees both authors' retreats as "a vantage point from which to criticize the life around them, which permitted them to search for reality in their own terms, and to conclude from that search that it is possible, if one grant respect and integrity to each, to heal the dichotomy between the physical and the spiritual."

10 EVANS, WILLIAM R. "Frost's Barding at Bates." *Dartmouth College Library Bulletin* 19 (November): 38-44.

On Frost's friendship with Bates graduate Sidney Cox and Cox's arrangement for Frost to read there in March 1916. "what won the audience . . . was Frost's sense of humor."

11 FINGER, LARRY L. "Frost's 'The Road Not Taken': A 1925 Letter Come to Light." *American Literature* 50 (November): 478-79.

Prints a letter Frost wrote to a young Tennessee girl, Chrystine Yates, answering her query about the "sigh" of the poem. Frost replied that it was a "private jest," nothing profound.

12 FLEISSNER, ROBERT F. "From 'Wooed' to Wood?: A Frost Debt to Beddoes Reconsidered." *English Language Notes* 15 (March): 208-10.

Reply to 1976.68. Finds no evidence that Robert Frost ever read Beddoes. Updated in 1988.13.

1978

13 ____. "Frost and Tennyson: New Points." *American Notes and Queries* 16 (January): 72-73.

Lists ten points of comparison to show a kinship to Tennyson, though not to Matthew Arnold or Robert Browning.

14 ____. "'Frost . . . at . . . Play': A Frost-Dickinson Affinity Affirmed." *Research Studies* (Washington State University) 46 (March): 28-39.

Finds parallels between Frost's "Fire and Ice" and Dickinson's "Death and Life" (or "Apparently with no surprise").

15 ____. "Frost's 'Acquainted with the Night.'" *Explicator* 37 (Fall): 12-13.

On the clock image in the poem and the possible clocks Frost may have had in mind.

16 FOSTER, CHARLES H. "Robert Frost at Bread Loaf." In *Frost: Centennial Essays III*. Edited by Jac Tharpe. Jackson: University Press of Mississippi, pp. 70-82.

Foster's diary from the summer of 1938 describes Frost after the death of his wife and Frost's view of himself as "a completely unforgivable, selfish husband." Describes several of Frost's talks at the Bread Loaf Writers' conference.

17 ____. "The Two Frosts and the Poetics of Confession." In *Frost: Centennial Essays III*. Edited by Jac Tharpe. Jackson: University Press of Mississippi, pp. 350-67.

Describes the "false" and the "true" poet, "the derivative young poet writing by the book versus the emerging unique voice and vision of the authentic Frost," which is signaled in "New Hampshire" in 1923.

18 FRANCIS, ROBERT. "Frost as Apple Peeler." *New England Review and Bread Loaf Quarterly* 1 (March): 32-39.

Defends his own poem, "Apple Peeler," in *New Poems by American Poets* (1953) against Frost's misinterpretation and consequent anger.

19 FRENCH, ROBERTS W. "Robert Frost and the Darkness of Nature." *English Record* (New York State English Council) 29 (Winter): 2-5.

On images of darkness in several of Frost's nature poems.

20 FRENCH, WARREN. "'The Death of the Hired Man': Modernism and Transcendence." In *Frost: Centennial Essays III*. Edited by Jac Tharpe: Jackson: University Press of Mississippi, pp. 382-401.

Describes views of Modernism in American literature. The five characters named or referred to in "The Death of the Hired Man" represent pre-Modernist, Modernist, and post-Modernist points of view.

21 FROST, LESLEY. "In Aladdin's Lamp Light." In *Frost: Centennial Essays III*. Edited by Jac Tharpe. Jackson: University Press of Mississippi, pp. 313-15.

Describes Frost's childhood reading and later readings for his own children. Affirms Frost's belief in God. Also: "Love, then, was the original source, the instinctual way, through nature, of being in touch with Divinity. Perhaps love *was* divinity."

*22 FUJIMOTO, MASAKI. "Kiki karano Dasshustsu: Frost-shi niokeru Chie eno Michi" [Escape from crisis: The way to wisdom in Frost's poems]. *Bungaku to Hyoron* (Japan) 10:34-41.

23 GOLDSTEIN, LAURENCE. "'Kitty Hawk' and the Question of American Destiny." *Iowa Review* 9 (Winter): 41-49.

"Writing 'Kitty Hawk' at the end of his career, Frost, his nation's unofficial Poet Laureate, aligned his vision with the orthodox American view of social evolution. Poets remain earthbound, yearning to penetrate out far and in deep. But in fact science, our greatness, can best play the heroic role which Fate has given the superior in spirit."

24 GUERNSEY, BRUCE HUBBARD. "The Ax, the Scythe, and the Pen: Work and Leisure in the Poetry of Robert Frost." *DAI* 39, 07A, p. 4256. Ph.D. dissertation, University of New Hampshire, 163 pp.

Sees the interrelationship of work and leisure in Frost's life and poetry as a process of "clearing," which he continually renews in his poems.

25 HALL, DONALD. "Vanity, Fame, Love, and Robert Frost." In *Remembering Poets: Reminiscences and Opinions: Dylan Thomas, Robert Frost, T. S. Eliot, and Ezra Pound*. New York: Harper and Row, pp. 39-75.

Recalls acquaintance with Frost for twenty years until Frost's death. "Over the years, he changed for me, from a monument to a public fraud to something more human and complicated than either praise or blame could deal with. When I look back now, with knowledge of the life he lived, I look at old scenes with new eyes."

1978

26 HALL, DOROTHY JUDD. "An Old Testament Christian." In *Frost: Centennial Essays II*. Edited by Jac Tharpe. Jackson: University Press of Mississippi, pp. 316-49.

Argues that Frost was religious, influenced primarily by the Bible and the philosophy of Henri Bergson, especially *Creative Evolution*, which helped "confirm his belief in the value of form-making as a human endeavor. To compose a poem is to join in spirit, he liked to think, with a greater creative power in the universe–call it (we may) the élan vital, or (he would prefer) God."

27 HASKELL, JOHN D., Jr. "Addendum to Van Egmond: Robert Frost." *Papers of the Bibliographical Society of America* 72 (July-September): 348.

Adds to item 1974.89: Vivian Savacool, "Books of New Hampshire Interest: *New Hampshire* by Robert Frost," *Granite Monthly* 56 (January 1924): 52-53.

28 HENRY, NAT. "Frost's 'Stopping by Woods on a Snowy Evening.'" *Explicator* 37 (Fall): 37-38.

Suggests that if the poem is about death, it is about "the *little death* of abnegation to which we sentence ourselves daily."

*29 HIGASHIYAMA, MASAYOSHI. "Frost no Tegami" [Frost's Letters]. In *Ashiya Daigaku Soritsu 15-shunen Kinen Ronbunshu* (Japan). Ashiya Daidaku, pp. 421-45.

*30 ISHIDO, TETSUYA. "Robert Frost no Shorter Poems ni tsuite" [Robert Frost's shorter poems]. *Bunka Kiyo* (Hirosdaki Daigaku Kyoyobu) (Japan) 12, no. 2:35-46.

31 LeVEE: LUELLA NASH. "Per Ardua as Astra." In *Frost: Centennial Essays III*. Edited by Jac Tharpe. Jackson: University Press of Mississippi, pp. 83-104.

Reminiscence of Frost and others who knew him, using the motif of stars in the poetry. "The most vivid symbols in his verse, stars also flashed in and out of his conversations and added brilliance to his conversation. It is said that, in all his travels in this country and abroad, he never went to sleep without first looking into the night sky for the North Star."

32 LITTLEFIELD, T.H. "A Ripton Afternoon." In *Frost: Centennial Essays III*. Edited by Jac Tharpe. Jackson: University Press of Mississippi, pp. 3-6.

Recalls a talk with Frost in Ripton, Vermont, and Frost's comments on other poets, particularly of an incident involving William Butler Yeats. Frost said: "But we're all damned liars, you know."

33 LORD, JOHN B., Sr. "Of Frost, Cats, Poetry, and Distinctive Feature Analysis." *Language and Style* 11 (Summer): 173-80.

Describes an aspect of Frost's linguistic study as a young man in his attempt to convey ordinary speaking into poetic language.

34 McGREGOR, ELISABETH JOHNSON. "The Poet's Bible: Biblical Elements in the Poetry of Emily Dickinson, Stephen Crane, Edwin Arlington Robinson, and Robert Frost." *DAI* 39, 10A, p. 6133. Ph.D. dissertation, Brown University, 298 pp.

Examines Frost's use of the Bible in his poetry. He "brought together biblical language and pastoralism to express his belief in the endurance of spiritual values, and at the same time to commemorate what he felt modern man had lost. With a mixture of critical wit and deep attachment to the Bible reminiscent of Dickinson's, he used it with subtlety and feeling which have gone largely unappreciated."

35 McKAY, JUDITH SUE. "Diminishment, Imagination, and Belief in the Poetry of Robert Frost." *DAI* 39, 06A, p. 3583. Ph.D. dissertation, University of Mississippi, 197 pp.

Examines the theme of "diminishment from the ideal"–"what to make of a diminished thing"–in Frost's poetry. Discusses the nature poems as imagination as a redemptive act. Sees the poetry as "acts which he apparently hoped would please God."

36 MILLER, LEWIS H., Jr. "William James, Robert Frost, and 'The Black Cottage.'" In *Frost: Centennial Essays III*. Edited by Jac Tharpe. Jackson: University Press of Mississippi, pp. 368-81.

Discusses the "affinities of temperament, tone, and thought pervasive in the work of the two men." Frost's poetic voice has "the homey, colloquial phrases and rhythms" of James's *Pragmatism: A New Name for Some Old Ways of Thinking*. Examines "The Black Cottage" in terms of voice and poetic meaning.

37 MONTEIRO, GEORGE. "Robert Frost's Dickinson Books." *Dickinson Studies*, no. 33, pp. 3-7.

Describes five books pertaining to Emily Dickinson's life and poetry given by Lesley Frost Ballantine to the Foles Library of New York University, of some three thousand volumes belonging to her father.

1978

*38 NARITA, MICHIKO. "'Boston no Kita' no Jikken: Shinrigeki ni tsuite" [Experiment of *North of Boston*: Psychological poems]. *Jissen Eibungaku* (Japan) 13:61-92

39 PERRINE, LAURENCE. "Frost's 'Acquainted with the Night.'" *Explicator* 37 (Fall): 13-14.

Argues that the "luminary clock" in the poem is really a clock, not the moon.

40 ____. "Frost's 'Provide, Provide.'" *Notes on Contemporary Literature* 8 (March): 9.

Reply to Philip Gerber (*Robert Frost*, Twayne, 1966). Corrects the "misreading " of the poem. Says the poem is ironic, "delivered in the tone of cynical worldly wisdom."

41 ____. "Letting Go With the Heart: Frost's 'Wild Grapes.'" *Notes on Modern American Literature* 2 (Summer): Item 20.

Reply to W.W. Robson (*Southern Review* 2 [1966]). Suggests Frost's meaning of "letting go" is a loving act, letting go with the mind but not the heart.

42 REICHERT, VICTOR E. "The Robert Frost I Knew." In *Frost: Centennial Essays III*. Edited by Jac Tharpe. Jackson: University Press of Mississippi, pp. 105-22.

An affectionate reminiscence of Frost's friendship with Rabbi Reichert. Examines Frost's statement: "You know, you haven't been a Jew for nothing." Discusses Frost's knowledge of the Scripture and religion.

43 REPLOGLE, JUSTIN. "Vernacular Poetry: Frost to Frank O'Hara." *Twentieth Century Literature* 24 (Summer): 137-53.

Provides a linguistic analysis of the speaking voice in the two poets. Discusses "The Housekeeper," "Wild Grapes," "Place for a Third," and "New Hampshire."

44 SLAKEY, ROGER L. "Frost's 'Moon Compasses.'" *Explicator* 37 (Fall): 22-23.

Reply to 1974.31. Suggests that the poem is not about circularity, but about "the caliper and metaphorically with its function."

45 STANLIS, PETER J. "Acceptable in Heaven's Sight: Frost at Bread Loaf: 1939-1941." In *Frost: Centennial Essays III*. Edited by Jac Tharpe. Jackson: University Press of Mississippi, pp. 179-311.

Reminiscence of Frost, presented "descriptively as a conversationalist," during a critical period in his career. Describes life at Bread Loaf and conversations with Frost and other teachers there. Corrects Lawrance Thompson's biographical interpretation of Frost as "a bad man" in those years.

46 STOUT, JANIS P. "Convention and Variation in Frost's Sonnets." *Concerning Poetry* 11 (Spring): 27-36.

Finds Frost's sonnets strongest when he varies the conventional pattern, and those "in which Frost least varies the conventions tend to be his weakest."

47 TAYLOR, ANYA. "A Reply to Robert Fleissner's 'From Wooed to Wood: A Frost Debt to Beddoes' Reconsidered." *English Language Notes* 15 (March): 211.

Reply to 1978.12. Defends the original argument that Frost might have read Beddoes's "The Phantom Wooer."

48 TEFS, WAYNE ARMIN. "The Agitated Heart: Frost's Psychological Themes." *DAI* 39, 05A, p. 2933. Ph.D. dissertation, University of Manitoba.

Examines the poems from a psychological perspective to discover an "abstracted structure," which is that "the central thread of Frost's poetry is the struggle to bring about a satisfactory relation between the exposed self and a foreboding reality through the creation of symbols of order."

49 THARPE, JAC [L.], ed. *Frost: Centennial Essays III*. Jackson: University Press of Mississippi, 408 pp.

Contents: T.H. Littlefield, "A Ripton Afternoon"; Dorothy Tyler, "Robert Frost in Michigan"; Charles H. Foster, "Robert Frost at Bread Loaf"; Luella Nash LeVee, "Per Ardua ad Astra"; Victor E. Reichert, "The Robert Frost I Knew"; Reginald L. Cook, "Robert Frost in Context"; N. Arthur Bleau, "Robert Frost's Favorite Poem"; Peter J. Stanlis, "Acceptable in Heaven's Sight: Robert Frost at Bread Loaf, 1939-1941"; Lesley Frost, "In Aladdin's Lamp Light"; Dorothy Judd Hall, "An Old Testament Christian"; Richard Foster, "The Two Frosts and the Poetics of Confession"; Lewis H. Miller, Jr., "William James, Robert Frost, and 'The Black Cottage'"; Warren French, "'The Death of the Hired Man': Modernism and Transcendence."

50 THOMPSON, ROBERT B. "Frost's 'Accidentally on Purpose.'" *Explicator* 36 (Winter): 17.

Suggests that Frost's "disbelief . . . signalizes the poet's move from romanticism towards existentialism."

51 TYLER, DOROTHY. "Robert Frost in Michigan." In *Frost: Centennial Essays III*. Edited by Jac Tharpe. Jackson: University Press of Mississippi, pp. 7-69.

Biographical account of Frost's association with the University of Michigan, especially the academic years 1921-22, 1922-23, and 1925-26. Recounts anecdotes, describes the Frosts' houses, and Frost's sittings for portraits. Contains photographs and other illustrations.

52 VAN DORE, WADE. "Poem Written on the Morning of 22 May 1977, for the Dedication of the Robert Frost Farm at Derry, New Hampshire." *Thoreau Journal Quarterly* 10 (July): 25.

Blank verse poem of twenty-four lines.

53 WEST, MICHAEL. "Versifying Thoreau: Frost's 'The Quest of the Purple-Fringed' and 'Fire and Ice.'" *English Language Notes* 16 (September): 40-47.

Suggests that both poems may be influenced by Thoreau's *Journals*, which "almost surely figured in [Carl] Burell's extensive botanical library," in which Frost read.

54 WYATT, DAVID M. "Frost's Modernity." *Virginia Quarterly Review* 54 (Spring): 356-60.

Review of 1977.30. Suggests that "loving explication is just what Poirier performs in order to restore Frost to the canon [of American literature]." Sees Frost as modern while still traditional.

55 YASINSKI, WILLIAM ARNOLD, Jr. "Robinson, Frost, and Aestheticism: The Imagination of Survival." *DAI* 39, 09A, p. 5519. Ph.D. dissertation, Indiana University, 307 pp.

Compares and contrasts the two poets based on the "general influences of such aestheticist thinkers and writers as Schopenhauer, Nietzsche, Rossetti, Pater, Swinburne, and Wilde."

1979

1 ABEL, DARREL. "Robert Frost's 'Flirting with the *Entelechies*.'" *Renascence* 32 (Autumn): 33-44.

On individualism, separatism, and social interaction in the poems.

2 ____. "Two Philosophical Poets: Frost, Emerson, and Pragmatism." *Emerson Society Quarterly* 25 (3d Quarter): 119-36.

On Emerson's early influence on Frost, who later became a "poetic philosopher" as a consequence of reading William James.

*3 ANDO, CHIYOKO. "Robert Frost no Shutoteki Sinnen: Shi wa Kami eno Sasagemono" [Robert Frost's religious belief: Poetry is an offering to God]. *Saniku Gakuin Tankidaigaku Kiyo* (Japan) 8:37-54.

4 ARMS, GEORGE, and NAT HENRY. "Frost's 'Mending Wall.'" *Explicator* 37 (Spring): 29-32.

On misreadings in the poem and misreadings of poetry in general.

5 BARBOUR, BRIAN. "Frost's 'Once by the Pacific.'" *Explicator* 37 (Summer): 18-19.

Disagrees with Reuben Brower's interpretation in *The Poetry of Robert Frost: Constellations of Intention* (1963). Sees the speaker's inability to predict the outcome of "Put out the light."

6 BENTLEY, LOUISE DAVIS. "Human Relationships in Robert Frost's Dialogue Poems." *DAI* 40, 05A, p. 2675. Doctor of Arts Dissertation, Middle Tennessee State University, 243 pp.

Discusses twenty-two poems as they illustrate various dialogues of "human beings interacting with other humans" in several sorts of situations.

7 BIEGANOWSKI, RONALD. "Frost's 'Desert Places.'" *Explicator* 38 (Fall): 20-21.

"Specifically, as a metaphor, desert places represent his expression, his having something to express, of himself. He comes upon a filament of subtlety within himself, upon his own substance, his soul."

8 ____. "Sense of Place and Religious Consciousness." In *Robert Frost: Studies of the Poetry*. Edited by Kathryn Gibbs Harris. Boston: G.K. Hall, pp. 29-47.

The New England world offered Frost "realms of the spirit." "Frost's concern for matters of the spirit continued throughout his lifetime as the ultimate focus of his poetry; it attests to his seriousness. The sense of place in his poetry embodies his religious consciousness in a way which insists upon the primary role of spirit for Frost. Just as his reliance upon place continues from his first poems to the last ones, so does his spiritual life unfold from his first entering the pasture to his last clearing of the spring."

9 BORROFF, MARIE. *Language and the Poet: Verbal Artistry in Frost, Stevens, and Moore*. Chicago: University of Chicago Press, 198 pp.

What is "literary and elevated" in Frost's poetry rises from simplicity. Includes 1971.3.

10 BRADLEY, DAVID (text), and DEWITT JONES (photographs). *Robert Frost: A Tribute to the Source*. New York: Holt, Rinehart and Winston, 165 pp.

Reprints Frost poems with color photographs and commentary.

11 CHALLENDER, CRAIG ALTON. "The Poetic Principle in the Poetry of Robert Frost." *DAI* 40, 02A, p. 849. Ph.D. dissertation, University of Oklahoma, 203 pp.

Suggests that Frost's poetic process "is characterized by a constant movement inward and downward. Dwelling deep within poems are resonances, densities, that inform the factuality of our everyday world and form the essence of our thoughts."

12 COOK, MARJORIE. "Detachment, Irony, and Commitment." In *Robert Frost: Studies of the Poetry*. Edited by Kathryn Gibbs Harris. Boston: G.K. Hall, pp. 49-62.

In his poetry Frost displays "the commitment and detachment of serious wit." He operates in three ways: presenting an ambiguity inherent to the human situation; showing ironic contrasts between the expected and the actual event, but without commenting; and then moving beyond them "to a commitment that incorporates and transcends the essential ambiguity."

13 CUBETA, PAUL M. "Robert Frost and Edward Thomas: Two Soldier Poets." *New England Quarterly* 52 (June): 147-76.

On Frost's best friendship of all, and the poetic influence on both men.

14 FINNEGAN, SISTER JEREMY. "Creative Borrowing: Auditory Memory and Latin Heritage." In *Robert Frost: Studies of the Poetry*. Edited by Kathryn Gibbs Harris. Boston: G.K. Hall, pp. 101-16.

On the echoes of Latin literature in the poetry. Also describes Frost's prodigious memory of British and American poetry. Quotes Dryden: "What would be theft in other poets is only victory in him."

15 FLEISSNER, ROBERT F. "A Road Taken: The Romantically Different *Ruelle*." In *Robert Frost: Studies of the Poetry*. Edited by Kathryn Gibbs Harris. Boston: G.K. Hall, pp. 117-31.

On Wordsworthian elements in "The Road Not Taken." Provides a textual comparison with "Song" (Wordsworth's title) or "She Dwelt Among the Untrodden Ways."

16 ____. "Robert Frost, "'Once by the Pacific': The Moorish Genesis." *CLA Journal* 23:160-71.

Examines the poem's well-known concluding line in view of comments by Frost friends and also finds evidence of Shakespeare's *Othello* in other poems.

17 FLINKER, NOAM. "Robert Frost's Masques: The Genre and the Poems." *Papers on Language and Literature* 15 (Winter): 59-72.

Discusses the masques and the three stages of the genre historically. Finds Frost's "are modifications of the Renaissance genre."

18 FOLSOM, MICHAEL. "Poets and Presidents: Frost and Lowell." *New Orleans Review* 5, no. 1:21-26.

Compares Frost and Robert Lowell as each accepted or rejected approbation from the White House.

19 FRANKLIN, ROSEMARY F. "Frost's 'Worn Book of Old Golden Song.'" *English Language Notes* 16 (June): 315-21.

On Frost's reading in Francis T. Palgrave's *Golden Treasury*, second series (1896), and possible echoes in his own poetry.

20 ____. "Literary Model for Frost's Suicide Attempt in the Dismal Swamp." *American Literature* 50 (January): 645-46.

Suggests Thomas Moore's "A Ballad: The Lake of the Dismal Swamp" (1803) as the possible source of Frost's dramatic gesture.

21 "Frost Memorabilia Donated for Archives." *Washington Post*, 3 January, Section B, p. 9.

UPI account of Frost's copy of *New Hampshire*, inscribed for his wife, his Pulitzer Prize diploma, and other memorabilia donated to the University of New Hampshire.

22 GERBER, PHILIP L. "Bound Away–and Back Again." In *Robert Frost: Studies of the Poetry*. Edited by Kathryn Gibbs Harris. Boston: G.K. Hall, pp. 65-75.

Frost presents problems and riddles without offering solutions. "If Frost's expression of ultimate goals does rest among his figures, it is hidden too cunningly for most of us to discern, concealed, as it were, behind the stones of some private wall he was unable to scale."

23 GREINER, DONALD J. "The Difference Made for Prosody." In *Robert Frost: Studies of the Poetry*. Edited by Kathryn Gibbs Harris. Boston: G.K. Hall, pp. 1-16.

On Frost's innovations within traditional poetic forms. Although he refused to join the advocates of the "new poetry"–Pound, Eliot, Stevens, for example–Frost "altered, nevertheless, many of the standard verse forms even as he insisted upon the need for traditional form in poetry."

24 GUIMOND, JAMES K. "*A Way Out*: Pastoral Psychodrama." In *Robert Frost: Studies of the Poetry*. Edited by Kathryn Gibbs Harris. Boston: G.K. Hall, pp. 133-41.

On the biographical and traditional pastoral elements in Frost's one-act play. The two characters in the play represent the two sides of Frost's ambivalent attitude toward farming and the academic life, in which the play conceals "a tense, difficult synthesis."

25 HARRIS, KATHRYN GIBBS. "Lyric Impulse: Birds and Other Voices." In *Robert Frost: Studies of the Poetry*. Boston: G.K. Hall, pp. 143-56.

As a "synecdochic symbolist," Frost uses birds in his poetry to parallel events in his life. Also analyzes Frost's poetic voices.

26 ____, ed. *Robert Frost: Studies of the Poetry*. Boston: G.K. Hall, 196 pp.

Contents: Donald J. Greiner, "The Difference Made for Prosody"; John A. Rea, "Language and Form in 'Nothing Gold Can Stay'"; Ronald Bieganowski, "Sense of Place and Religious Consciousness"; Marjorie Cook, "Detachment, Irony, and Commitment"; Philip L. Gerber, "Bound Away–And Back Again"; Clifford Lyons, "'Not Unbounded'"; William A. Sutton, "Problems of Biography"; Peter Van Egmond, "A Note on Bibliographical Problems"; Sister Jeremy Finnegan, "Creative Borrowing: Auditory Memory and Latin Heritage"; Robert F. Fleissner, "A Road Taken: The Romantically Different *Ruelle*"; James K. Guimond, "*A Way Out*: Pastoral Psychodrama"; Kathryn G. Harris, "Lyric Impulse: Birds and Other Voices"; Nancy C. Joyner, "Comic Exegete"; James F. Knapp,

"The Greek World and the Mystery of Being"; Mordecai Marcus, "Psychoanalytic Approaches to 'Mending Wall.'"

27 ____. "Two Difficult Biographies of Robert Frost." *Literature and Psychology* 29, nos. 1-2:19-24.

Describes difficulties in writing the biography of a contemporary, using Lawrance Thompson's work and Robert S. Newdick's as examples.

28 JOYNER, NANCY C. "Comic Exegete." In *Robert Frost: Studies of the Poetry*. Edited by Kathryn Gibbs Harris. Boston: G.K. Hall, pp. 143-56.

On Frost's biblical references in the comic and the serious poems. "The jokes Frost makes about the Bible are aimed not so much at the Bible itself but at the received interpretation of it; thus he poses as the inept exegete for the very serious reason of exposing inconsistencies in people's attitudes towards the myth. More importantly, he treats the Bible humorously in order to achieve an aesthetic distance from his subject matter."

29 KEMP, JOHN C. *Robert Frost and New England: The Poet as Regionalist*. Princeton, N.J.: Princeton University Press, 273 pp.

On Frost as a New Englander and the several ways it affected his poetry as an outsider looking in. Argues that Frost's unwillingness to change his persona was a detriment in his later work.

30 KNAPP, JAMES F. "The Greek World and the Mystery of Being." In *Robert Frost: Studies of the Poetry*. Edited by Kathryn Gibbs Harris. Boston: G.K. Hall, pp. 165-78.

On the influence of Greek philosophy, literature, and mythology on the poetry. "But his love for the early Greek world was also a part of his struggle to seize life in a deadening time, and it was akin to the endeavor of Modernist thought in writers as different as Martin Heidegger and T.S. Eliot, Ezra Pound and D.H. Lawrence: to make some part of the distant past new, and so redeem the present."

31 LYONS, CLIFFORD. "'Not Unbounded.'" In *Robert Frost: Studies of the Poetry*. Edited by Kathryn Gibbs Harris. Boston: G.K. Hall, pp. 77-87.

The walls, boundaries, and other restraints in Frost's poetry do not necessarily confine him or us. "We have the best of all freedoms – to make and find form and meaning, not only in art but in the many endeavors of our lives as well. It is bounds that make attainments possible; bonds need not be bondage."

1979

32 MARCUS, MORDECAI. "Psychoanalytic Approaches to 'Mending Wall.'" In *Robert Frost: Studies of the Poetry*. Edited by Kathryn Gibbs Harris. Boston: G.K. Hall, pp. 179-90.

On how psychoanalysis, including the psychosexual, may be used to interpret some of the poems, particularly "Mending Wall." Applies Erik H. Erikson's theory of eight developmental stages of human life to the poem: oral sensory: basic trust versus mistrust; muscular-anal: autonomy versus shame and doubt; locomotor-genital: initiative versus guilt; latency: industry versus inferiority; puberty and adolescence: identity versus role confusion; young adulthood: intimacy versus isolation; adulthood: generativity versus stagnation; maturity: ego integrity versus despair.

33 MARTIN, DALE FREDERICK. "Robert Frost: The Poet as Mythmaker." *DAI* 40, 02A, pp. 854-55. Ph.D. dissertation, Southern Illinois University (Carbondale), 146 pp.

Discusses Frost's New England as a mythic landscape that is inclusive and makes him a major poet and a modern one.

34 MORTON, BRUCE. "Addenda and Amendments to Lentricchia's *Robert Frost*." *Papers of the Bibliographical Society of America* 73:120-21.

Adds seventeen items of primary and secondary interest to 1976.33. Offers several corrections as well.

35 MULDER, WILLIAM. "Seeing 'New-Englandly': Planes of Perception in Emily Dickinson and Robert Frost." *New England Quarterly* 52 (December): 550-59.

A comparison-contrast of the two poets' vision of their locale at various levels. For Dickinson it was "beatific and agonized"; for Frost, "pastoral and stoic, courageously humanistic."

*36 ONJOHJI, YASUKO. "Frost no Gekishi no Onnatachi: Jiga no Hokai" [Women in Frost's dramatic poems: Collapse of ego]. *Tokyo Seitoku Tankigaigaku Kiyo* 12:41-47.

*37 ____. "On the Modernity of Frost's Dramatic Poems." *Researcher* (Japan) 9:83-97.

38 OSTER, JUDITH AGNES LINK. "Nature and Man in the Poetry of Robert Frost." *DAI* 40, 05A, p. 2685. Ph.D. dissertation, Case Western Reserve University, 314 pp.

Examines Frost's poetry as "man *defining* himself in relation to nature. At the heart of his poetic drama is the duality he feels inherent in all life, and the resulting tensions require keeping the opposing sides in balance."

39 PEARLMAN, DANIEL. "Frost and the Work Ethic: A Reading of 'Two Tramps in Mud Time.'" *Modernist Studies: Literature and Culture* 3, no. 2:61-68.

Finds Frost's real attitude in the poem was influenced by the "welfare mentality of the Thirties" . . . that contradicted New England self-reliance.

40 ____. "A Political Satire Unveiled: Frost's 'Neither Out Far Nor In Deep.'" *Agenda* (London) 17 (Summer): 41-63.

Suggests that the poem is a veiled comment on the Franklin D. Roosevelt administration and its "reign of terror . . . against all manifestations of political conservatism during the period of the New Deal."

41 PERRINE, LAURENCE. "Frost's 'Iris by Night.'" *Concerning Poetry* 12 (Spring): 35-43.

Suggests "the poem celebrates Frost's friendship with Edward Thomas." Provides a thorough analysis, thematically and metrically.

42 ____. "Frost's 'The Span of Life.'" *Explicator* 37 (Summer): 4.

Disagrees with Richard Eberhart (*Southern Review*, n.s. 2 [1966]). Sees the dog as friendly, not hostile.

43 POLLOCK, JOHN J. "Dante and Frost's 'Stopping by Woods.'" *Notes on Contemporary Literature* 9 (March): 5.

Suggests that the poem echoes the first book of *The Divine Comedy*.

44 REA, JOHN A. "Language and Form in 'Nothing Gold Can Stay.'" In *Robert Frost: Studies of the Poetry*. Edited by Kathryn Gibbs Harris. Boston: G.K. Hall, pp. 17-25.

An exhaustive analysis of the poem, its various versions, and the explications of those versions. "Poetic and linguistic form help Robert Frost impose order on the apparent chaos of the universe and of language by letting him find and arrange their underlying patterns into a bit of human neatness in the relentless wilderness. 'After making a poem,' he said, 'you have no right to boast of anything but the form.'"

1979

45 REID, B.L. "Four Winds." *Sewanee Review* 87 (Spring): 273-88.
On visits with Dylan Thomas, Frost, Eliot, and Pound. Only three paragraphs describing Frost and a reading at Amherst in October 1962.

46 ROOD, KAREN LANE. "Robert Frost before England: The Development of a Modern Poet, 1890-1912." *DAI* 40, 03A, p. 1473. Ph.D. dissertation, University of South Carolina, 404 pp.
Examines the influence of Francis Turner Palgrave's *The Golden Treasury of the Best Songs and Lyrical Ballads* (1861) on Frost's poetry. Also sees the influence of William James.

*47 SAWADA, SUKETARO. "Robert Frost niokeru 'Chie': Yuki to Ai no Shinwa" ["Wisdom" in Robert Frost: The myth of love and courage]. *Gifu Joshi Daigaku Kiyo* (Japan) 8:105-14.

48 SCHEELE, ROY. "Source and Resource: A Stylistic Note on Frost's 'Spring Pools.'" *Papers on Language and Literature* 15 (Summer): 316-19.
Suggests that Frost's source is Tennyson's *The Lady of Shalott*.

49 SHARP, RONALD A. "Robert Frost at Midnight." *Papers on Language and Literature* 15 (Summer): 311-16.
Finds Frost's "An Old Man's Winter Night" "his own darkly ironic version" of Coleridge's "Frost at Midnight."

50 SUTTON, WILLIAM A. "Problems of Biography." In *Robert Frost: Studies of the Poetry*. Edited by Kathryn Gibbs Harris. Boston: G.K. Hall, pp. 89-93.
On the inadequacies of Frost biographies at that time. Analyzes Lawrance Thompson's resentment because of Frost's unreliability as his primary source of information. Offers the conjecture: "Threatened as he was by Frost's invitation [to be his biographer] to [Louis] Untermeyer, he may have been afraid to do penetrating research, afraid Frost might have felt threatened and broken off their relationship, thereby tarnishing Thompson's scholarly reputation."

51 TEFS, WAYNE. "Measures as Counter Measures: The Function of Form in Frost's Poetry." *Gypsy Scholar* 6: 3-17.
Suggests that Frost, "seeing–the world as he did in terms of large inhuman forces threatening to overwhelm small things (like a human personality), [he] used form as a psychological strategy to resist the dangers of existence."

52 VAN EGMOND, PETER. "A Note on Bibliographical Problems." In *Robert Frost: Studies of the Poetry*. Edited by Kathryn Gibbs Harris. Boston: G.K. Hall, pp. 95-97.

Describes the need for a higher level of understanding and interpretation of Frost's poetry, especially in terms of biographical information. Describes the problem of scattered primary material and unique items (letters, tape-recorded talks and interviews, and similar things), in particular.

53 VOGT, VICTOR E. "Narrative and Drama in the Lyric: Robert Frost's Strategic Withdrawal." *Critical Inquiry* 5 (Spring): 529-51.

Analyzes "The Death of the Hired Man" to show "that one of Frost's presumed limitations, the strategic withdrawal implicit in his lack of interest in the story for its own sake, has in fact been creatively transformed into a strategic advance, realizing new potentials for the lyric genre."

54 VON FRANK, ALBERT J. "Frost's 'The Gift Outright.'" *Explicator* 38 (Fall): 22-23.

Suggests Marlowe's *Doctor Faustus* as the source for "the deed of gift."

55 WILSON, DOUGLAS L. "The Other Side of the Wall." *Iowa Review* 10 (Winter): 65-75.

Suggests that Frost's personal experience would have made him see the necessity and security of walls in "Mending Wall."

1980

1 ABEL, DARREL. "The Instinct of a Bard: Robert Frost on Science, Logic, and Poetic Truth." *Essays in Arts and Sciences* 9 (May): 59-75.

Shows the influence of William James and Henri Bergson on Frost's conception of poetic truth.

2 _____. "Robert Frost's 'Second-Highest Heaven.'" *Colby Library Quarterly* 16 (June): 78-90.

Suggests such a "heaven" is "a world of indetermination confined by necessity." Sees the influence of Blaise Pascal, Emerson, William James, and Henri Bergson on this notion in Frost's poetry.

3 ANGYAL, ANDREW. "Literary Politics and the Shaping of the Frost Poetic Canon." *South Carolina Review* 12 (Spring): 47-55.

Describes Frost's omission of certain poems from the *Complete Poems* and provides evidence of the need for a Frost variorum edition.

4 BIEGANOWSKI, RONALD. "Robert Frost's 'An Encounter.'" *Notes on Contemporary Literature* 10 (March): 4-5.

Suggests that the poem "contains Frost's literary criticism which identifies his way of knowing."

5 BRIGGS, CHRISTINE A. "The Dramatic Monologue in Robert Frost's 'The Pauper Witch of Grafton.'" *Ball State University Forum* 21 (Spring): 48-53.

Compares Frost's poem to Robert Browning's in his dramatic monologues. Analyzes the motives of the characters in the poem.

6 CLAUSEN, CHRISTOPHER. "Robert Frost's Marriage Group." *New England Review and Bread Loaf Quarterly* 2 (September): 466-77.

Describes marriage as a theme in Frost's poetry. Finds that it is "as varied and subtle a treatment of that universal theme as one can find anywhere in modern poetry."

7 CUNNINGHAM, DONALD BRUCE. "The Lurking Frost: Poet and Narrator in Six Poems by Robert Frost." *DAI* 40, 08A, p. 4594. Ph.D. dissertation, University of Nebraska, 148 pp.

Examines "Mending Wall," "The Road Not Taken," "Into My Own," "The Wood-Pile," "Two Tramps in Mud Time," and "The Need of Being Versed in Country Things" as representing Frost's hiding himself behind a narrator for manipulation of his material.

8 D'AVANZO, MARIO L. "Frost's 'Sand Dunes' and Thoreau's *Cape Cod.*" *Notes on Contemporary Literature* 10 (November): 2-4.

Hypothesizes "that *Cape Cod* provided a theme, diction, a variety of naturalistic detail, and an attitude which Frost distilled into poetic form."

9 EBERWEIN, JANE DONAHUE. "'The Wind's Will': Another View of Frost and Longfellow." *Colby Library Quarterly* 16 (September): 177-81.

Explores the significance of Frost's selection from Longfellow for the title of *A Boy's Will*.

10 EDWARDS, C. HINES, Jr. "Time and Structure in Frost's 'Acquainted with the Night.'" *Notes on Modern American Literature* 4 (Summer): Item 17.

Analyzes structure and arrangement to show their contribution to meaning.

11 FLEISSNER, ROBERT F. "Frost and Lanier: An Immediate Literary Source of 'Once by the Pacific.'" *Papers on Language and Literature* 16 (Summer): 320-25.

Finds parallels to Sidney Lanier's "Dark Night," though both poems also reflect Shakespeare's *Othello*.

12 ____. "A Possible Source for 'Forgive, O Lord.'" *Notes on Contemporary Literature* 10 (September): 9-10.

Suggests that the source is Tennyson's *In Memoriam*, "Prologue," stanzas 8-9.

*13 FUJIMOTO, MASAKI. "'Ariel Gata' kara 'Prospero Gata' e: Shijin Frost no Hensen" [From "Ariel type" to "Prospero type": Frost's change as a poet]. *Bungaku to Hyoron* (Japan) 14:52-66.

*14 ____. "Frost Shi niokeru Pastoral no Kozo: 'Boston no Kita' o Chushin ni" [Pastoral Structure in Frost's poems: *North of Boston*]. *Osaka Ongaku Daigaku Kenkyu Kiyo* (Japan) 19:103-22.

*15 HARADA, ASAKICHI. "A Broken Goblet: Frost no 'Directive' ni tsuite" [A broken goblet: On Frost's "Directive"]. *Mukogawa Joshi Daigaku Kiyo Bungakubu Hen* (Japan) 28:17-26.

*16 HIGASHIYAMA, MASAYOSHI. "Frost no Shi" [Frost's poems]. *Ashiya Daigaku Ronso* (Japan) 5:1-22.

17 JENKINS, R.B. "Robert Frost and the 'Agitated Heart.'" *Notes on Contemporary Literature* 10 (March): 7-10.

Describes Frost's theme of alienation and "the importance Frost places on human ties and associations."

18 KEITH, W.J. "Robert Frost." In *The Poetry of Nature: Rural Perspectives in Poetry from Wordsworth to the Present*. Toronto: University of Toronto Press, pp. 119-40.

Includes Frost in a study of British poets because of his association with England and because he revivified the poetry of the nineteenth century.

19 KELLY, WILLIAM J. "Frost's 'Out, Out–.'" *Explicator* 38 (Spring): 12-13.

Discusses the saw as a beastlike creature in the poem.

20 LEA, SYDNEY. "From Sublime to Rigamarole: Relations of Frost to Wordsworth." *Studies in Romanticism* (Boston) 19 (Spring): 83-108.

Compares such Wordsworth poems as *The Prelude*, "Michael," and "Ode to Duty" to several of Frost's.

21 LIEBMAN, SHELDON W. "Robert Frost: On the Dialectics of Poetry." *American Literature* 52 (May): 264-78.

Attempts to examine Frost's "statements on poetry and to suggest that they should be taken seriously." Examines devices in the poetry, such as metaphor and parable.

22 LIND, L.R. "Robert Frost, Classicist." *Classical and Modern Literature* 1 (Fall): 7-23.

Examines Frost's classical elements in the poetry as: "A. non-structural, limited, or simply contributing to the pattern of the poem, and B. structural or integral." Deals with a wide range of poems.

23 McMAHON, WILLIAM E. "The Symbolic Vistas of Frost and Stevens." *College Literature* 7 (Spring): 146-52.

Suggests that "their vistas are something like synecdoches of cosmic and metaphysical design. . . . Vistas operate much like setting, and a vista might be defined as a part of setting that can be imagined as a single visual event."

*24 ONJOHJI, YASUKO. "Frost niokeru Shi" [Death in Frost]. *Tokyo Seitoku Tankidaigaku Kiyo* 13:21-26.

25 PERRINE, LAURENCE. "Frost's 'Pod of the Milkweed.'" *Notes on Modern American Literature* 5 (Winter): Item 5.

On Frost's images of flowers and butterflies and their significance throughout the poetry.

26 ____. "Frost's 'The Telephone.'" *Notes on Contemporary Literature* 10 (May): 11-12.

Analyzes the two lovers who speak in the poem. They are "dramatically differentiated – the male ardent, fanciful, playful, but also diffident; the female more down to earth, but open and responsive."

27 ____. "A House for Frost's 'White-Tailed Hornet.'" *Notes on Contemporary Literature* 10 (January): 3.

Describes the natural process hornets follow in constructing their nests.

28 POTTER, JAMES L. *Robert Frost Handbook*. University Park: Pennsylvania University Press, 205 pp.

Attempts "to furnish the kind and the amount of background information and critical analysis of the poetry that will be useful to general readers or students who have Frost's work at hand." Part 1: Life and Works; part 2: Poetic Stance; part 3: Literary Contexts and Techniques.

29 PRATT, LINDA RAY. "Robert Frost and the Limits of Thought." *Arizona Quarterly* 36 (Autumn): 240-60.

Deals with the question of the nature and use of thought in Frost's poetry. Finds that "its damaging limitations are apparent when we compare Frost to other poets," Emily Dickinson and Wallace Stevens, for example.

30 ROSENDORF, VALERIE, and WILLIAM FREEDMAN. "Frost's 'Out, Out–.'" *Explicator* 39 (Fall): 10-11.

Describes parallels between the poem and the images of the Passion of Christ.

31 SCHULHOF, SAUNDRA ALICIA LEE. "Robert Frost: A Study of Marriage in His Life and in His Poetry." *DAI* 42, 04A, pp. 1639-1640. Ph.D. dissertation, Ball State University, 179 pp.

On Frost's treatment of communication, escape-return, sexism, and love in Frost's life and poetry. Sees marriage as a major influence.

32 SHENK, ROBERT. "Robert Frost and the Early Puritan Idea of Vocation." *Christian Scholars Review* 10, no. 3:229-37.

Suggests that Frost's idea of man's vocation has discernible antecedents in the writings of early English and American Puritans. Focuses on "Two Tramps in Mud Time" and "The Wood-Pile."

33 TAKEDA, MASAKO. "Robert Frost: Kamoku to Jozetsu" [Robert Frost: Taciturnity and talkativeness]. In *Suga Yasuo, Ogashi Kazugo: Ryokyoju Taikan Kinen Ronbunshu*. Kyoto: Apollonsha, pp. 876-88.

On taciturnity and talkativeness in the poetry.

34 TOLES, GEORGE E. Review of *Robert Frost and New England: The Poet as Regionalist*, by John C. Kemp. *New England Quarterly* 53 (June): 252-54.

See 1979.29. This study "offers a thorough and conscientious exploration of an intriguing, but not startlingly adventurous thesis."

35 WADDELL, WILLIAM S., Jr. "Aphorism in Robert Frost's 'The Tuft of Flowers': The Sound of Certainty." *Concerning Poetry* 13 (Spring): 41-44.

On the two well-known statements about work in the poem.

*36 WATANABE, SEIKO. "Robert Frost no Taiwageki" [Robert Frost's dialogue poems]. *Nihon Joshi Daigaku Eibei Bungaku Kenkyu* (Japan) 15:151-63.

37 WATSON, DOUGLAS FRANK. "A Sense of Place in the Poetry of Robert Frost, William Carlos Williams, and Wallace Stevens." *DAI* 41, 07A, p. 3111. Ph.D. dissertation, Texas Tech University, 238 pp.

Examines the functions as "setting and subject in the poetry of Frost, as subject (locus) in the poetry of Williams, and as vehicle in the poetry of Stevens."

38 WYATT, DAVID. "Frost and the Grammar of Motion." *Southern Review* (January): 86-99.

Suggests that "Frost's poems typically image a speaker or character performing a physical action which we can actually map out. Even when the act is one of the mind–a thought–Frost usually embodies it in a sequence of gestures we can visualize." Discusses "The Wood-Pile" and other poems.

*39 YOSHIMURA, KIYOSHI. "Yugen to Mugen: Robert Frost no Shizenkan, 1" [The finite and the infinite: Robert Frost's view of nature, 1]. *Chukyo Daigaku Bungakubu Kiyo* (Japan) 15:49-83.

1981

1 ABEL, DARREL. "'Unfriendly Nature' in the Poetry of Robert Frost." *Colby Library Quarterly* 17 (December): 201-10.

Describes hostile nature as a theme in several of the poems.

2 BASSETT, PATRICK F. "Frost's 'The Road Not Taken.'" *Explicator* 39 (Spring 1981): 41-43.

On the persona in the poem, who is Frost's "alter ego," seeking "a direction but discovers and speaks only the lie."

3 BENOIT, RAYMOND. "Folklore by Frost: 'Paul's Wife.'" *Notes on Modern American Literature* 5 (Fall): Item 22.

Applies T.S. Eliot's "objective correlative" to Frost's poem.

4 BIEGANOWSKI, RONALD. "*North of Boston*: Human Dimensions to Robert Frost's Spiritual Realm." In *Robert Frost: The Man and the Poet*. Edited by Earl J. Wilcox. Winthrop Studies on Major Modern Writers. Rock Hill, S.C.: Winthrop College, pp. 83-96.

Suggests that the book "records Frost's adventure into the human realm." It "begins with entry into the pasture, emphasizes human companionship, and leads ultimately toward the boundless."

5 BOBER, NATALIE. *A Restless Spirit: The Story of Robert Frost*. Introduction by Robin Hudnut. New York: Atheneum Press, 197 pp.

A biography for young people.

6 BROOKS, CLEANTH. "Frost and Nature." In *Robert Frost: The Man and the Poet*. Edited by Earl J. Wilcox. Winthrop Studies on Major Modern Writers. Rock Hill, S.C.: Winthrop College, pp. 1-18.

Suggests that Frost's "view is that nature is not aware that the human world exists at all: nature is deaf and dumb to all human aspirations." Concludes that "Frost neither worships nature nor fears her."

7 CHAVKIN, ALLAN. "The Ordering of the Sequence of Meditative Lyrics in Frost's *North of Boston*." *Markham Review* 10 (Summer): 67-68.

Describes the "three crucial meditative poems, 'Mending Wall,' 'After Apple-Picking,' and 'The Wood-Pile,'" as showing "the development in the attitude of the speaker . . . to the problem of man's alienation, the central preoccupation of the volume."

8 COOK, MARJORIE E. "Dilemmas of Interpretation: Ambiguities and Practicalities." In *Robert Frost: The Man and the Poet*. Edited by Earl J. Wilcox. Winthrop Studies on Major Modern Writers. Rock Hill, S.C.: Winthrop College, pp. 125-41.

Attempts to provide groundwork for understanding Frost's position in "the intellectual milieu of the late nineteenth and early twentieth centuries," and conflicting philosophical viewpoints. Frost's view of these is "not as dogma, but with an inner humor, detachment, broad perspective, ironic consciousness–and, for some few loves, with a full commitment beyond irony, in spite of irony."

1981

9 DAVISON, PETER. "Robert Frost: The Cost of Friendship." *Washington Post Book World*, 5 July, pp. 6-7.

Review of *Robert Frost and Sidney Cox: Forty Years of Friendship*, by William R. Evans (1981.13). Compares Frost to a heavyweight champion in his correspondence with Cox, a Golden Glove aspirant.

10 EDWARDS, C. HINES, Jr. "Frost's 'Once by the Pacific.'" *Explicator* 39 (Summer): 28-29.

Reply to 1979.5. Offers more evidence to support the idea that the poem is "blasphemous."

11 EVANS, OLIVER H. "'Deeds that Count': Robert Frost's Sonnets." *Texas Studies in Language and Literature* 23 (Spring): 123-37.

Analyzes Frost's use of the traditional sonnet form and his innovations and license within the form.

12 EVANS, WILLIAM R. "Frost's 'Sound of Sense' and a Popular Audience." *American Literature* 53 (March): 116-23.

Describes an interlude of Frost and his friend Sidney Cox. Prints a newly-discovered letter by Cox to his family in 1916, describing in detail Frost's reading and his ideas about poetry.

13 ____. *Robert Frost and Sidney Cox: Forty Years of Friendship*. Hanover, N.H.: University Press of New England, 297 pp.

On the lasting friendship of Frost and a fellow teacher, until Cox's death in 1952 at age 62.

14 FINGER, LARRY L. "That Frost Letter: Another Look." *CEA Critic* 43 (March): 36-39.

Refers to 1978.11. Concludes: "Not instinct, nor impulse, nor reason, but intuition led Frost to England, where he took his chances, once and for all, with poetry."

15 FLEISSNER, ROBERT F. "Frost and Keats: Sharers of Intensity." *Notes on Contemporary Literature* 11 (March): 2-4.

Suggests that there are several echoes of Keats's poetry in Frost's.

16 ____. "Frost's 'Fireflies in the Garden.'" *Explicator* 39 (Summer): 26-28.

On Frost's interest in the poetry of Gerard Manley Hopkins and the possible influence of his "The Starlight Night."

1981

17 FOLKES, JOHN COURTNEY. "The Function of Personality, Narrative Voice, Images, and Symbolism in the Poetry of Robert Frost." *DAI* 42, 10A, p. 4447. Ph.D. dissertation, University of Toronto, n.p.

Deals with the four functions as they "indicate overt meanings, unapparent and hitherto unidentified implications, authorial attitudes, subtle techniques and problematical situations in the poetry."

18 FRANCIS, LESLEY LEE. "Robert Frost and Majesty of Stones upon Stones." *Journal of Modern Literature* 9, no. 1:3-26.

Describes Frost's treatment of stones and Native American and South American Indians.

19 FUNKHOUSER, LINDA BRADLEY. "Acoustic Rhythm in Frost's 'Dust of Snow.'" *Language and Style* 14 (Fall): 287-303.

Analyzes the poem in terms of linguistic science.

20 GAGE, JOHN T. "Humour en Garde: Comic Saying in Robert Frost's Poetic." *Thalia* (University of Ottawa) 4 (Spring-Summer): 54-61.

Discusses Frost as humorist and "a master of both the direct and the indirect humorous assault" . . . that plays a central role in his poetics as a whole.

21 GLENN, BARBARA. "The Way Up and the Way Down: A Consideration of Robert Frost in the Context of Baudelaire and Emerson." *Southern Review* 17 (January): 142-63.

Describes Frost's place in "the modern tradition in which Baudelaire and Emerson are seminal figures."

22 GREINER, DONALD J. "Factual Men and Imagining Rabbits: Robert Frost and Wallace Stevens." In *Robert Frost: The Man and the Poet*. Edited by Earl J. Wilcox. Winthrop Studies on Major Modern Writers. Rock Hill, S.C.: Winthrop College, pp. 61-67.

Compares Frost's "An Old Man's Winter Night" with Stevens' "A Rabbit as the King of Ghosts." Suggests that "both poets insist upon a balance between ideas about the thing and the thing itself."

23 HARD, WALTER. "Medical Aid." In *Brand-X Anthology of Poetry*. Edited by William Zaranka. Cambridge, Mass.: Apple-Wood Books, pp. 262-63.

A poem parodying "Mending Wall."

1981

24 HAYS, PETER L. "Frost and the Critics: More Revelation on 'All Revelation.'" *English Language Notes* 18 (June): 283-90.

Offers an interpretation of the poem as "a cathode ray tube illuminating crystals within the geode as an accurate description of a television picture tube. . . . In language, tone, and imagery, I see the poem as an attack on those who take their knowledge of nature indirectly from television, 'all revelation' through any mechanical medium and not from first-hand experience."

25 HELPHINSTINE, FRANCES. "Frost's 'Two Look at Two.'" *Explicator* 39 (Summer): 31-33.

Describes Old Testament elements in the poem, especially images from the Song of Solomon.

26 HIGASHIYAMA, MASAYOSHI. *America Bungaku to Shizen: Thoreau to Frost* [American Literature and Nature: Thoreau and Frost]. Tokyo: Nanundo, 170 pp.

Sees Frost, like Emerson and Thoreau, starting from a Protestant view of God, becoming transcendentalist, then finally convinced of God, the Creator of all nature. Sees Frost's use of synecdoche as finding a certain aspect of God by poetically observing certain objects in nature.

*27 KANEYAMA, KATSUYA. "Robert Frost no Jojo no Tokushitsu: W.B. Yeats to Hikakushite" [Lyrical quality of Robert Frost: Compared to W.B. Yeats]. *Seishu Tankidaigaku Kenkyukiyo* (Japan) 12:56-64.

*28 ____. "Robert Frost no Shizenkan: Shishu 'A Boy's Will' ni tsuite" [Robert Frost's view of nature: On *A Boy's Will*]. *Hokkaido America Bungaku* (Nihon America Bungakkai Hokkaido Shibu) (Japan) 5:1-9.

29 LABIN, LINDA L. "The Whale and the Ash-Heap: Transfigurations of Jonah and Job in Modern American Literature: Frost, MacLeish, and Vonnegut." *DAI* 41, 11A, p. 4713. Ph.D. dissertation, Kent State University, 328 pp.

Compares Frost's depiction of Jonah and Job in the masques to those of Archibald MacLeish and Kurt Vonnegut.

30 LEGRIS, MAURICE. "The Joyful Killer of 'The Witch of Coös.'" *Studies in Humanities* 9 (December): 30-32.

Discusses the derivations of *Toffile* and *Lajway* to suggest "devil" and "joyful" as contributing further to the meaning of the poem.

31 LYONS, CLIFFORD. "Walks and Talks with Robert Frost." In *Robert Frost: The Man and the Poet*. Edited by Earl J. Wilcox. Winthrop Studies on Major Modern Writers. Rock Hill, S.C.: Winthrop College, pp. 69-81.

Provides "cumulative snapshots" in a reminiscence of Frost from a twenty-five-year friendship, beginning in 1931.

*32 MARCHANT, FREDERICK JOHN. "Getting Started: A Study of the Early Years of Robert Frost, William Carlos Williams, and Wallace Stevens." AAC0361712. Ph.D. dissertation, University of Chicago.

33 MASON, JULIAN. "'Out of the Air': The Friendship of Robert Frost and Lewis Chase." In *Robert Frost: The Man and the Poet*. Edited by Earl J. Wilcox. Winthrop Studies on Major Modern Writers. Rock Hill, S.C.: Winthrop College, pp. 97-114.

Describes Frost's friendship and correspondence with Chase, a professor of English, beginning in 1917 and surprisingly not mentioned in Lawrance Thompson's biography.

34 MONTEIRO, GEORGE. "Goring the Ox: Robert Frost, Robert Francis, and the Intentional Fallacy." In *Robert Frost: The Man and the Poet*. Edited by Earl J. Wilcox. Winthrop Studies on Major Modern Writers. Rock Hill, S.C.: Winthrop College, pp. 31-37.

Suggests that "The Road Not Taken" produced a reply by Francis in his "Apple Peeler," which in turn resulted in Frost's "After Apple-Picking," all revealing "hidden intentions" by both poets.

35 MORSE, SAMUEL FRENCH. "Robert Frost: Society and Solitude." In *American Literature: The New England Heritage*. Edited by James Nagel and Richard Astro. New York: Garland Publishing Co., pp. 131-43.

Demonstrates the influence of Emerson on Frost's poetry.

*36 NAKAMURA, ISAO. "Frost no Gendaisei" [Modernity of Frost]. *Aoyama Gakuin Daigaku Ippankyoiku Bukai Ronshu* (Japan) 22:137-46.

37 NITCHIE, GEORGE W. "Frost and the Unwritten Epic." In *Robert Frost: The Man and the Poet*. Edited by Earl J. Wilcox. Winthrop Studies on Major Modern Writers. Rock Hill, S.C.: Winthrop College, pp. 39-48.

Suggests that "American epic is loser's epic" and that Frost found no worthy epic subjects except himself, but "he did not make the final identification of himself with his own heroic darkness."

38 OELSCHLAGER, FRITZ H. "Tragic Vision in Frost's 'Home Burial.'" *Ball State University Forum* 22 (Summer): 25-29.

Suggests that the wife's "denunciation of the world's evil should not be easily dismissed as the product of 'intermittent mental sickness.' Amy may, in fact, be mad, but such madness is that of the tragic figure raging against an arbitrary universe."

*39 ONJOHJI, YASUKO. "Frost niokeru Shi" [Death in Frost]. *Tokyo Seitoku Tankigaidaku Kiyo* 14:57-62.

40 PARINI, JAY. "Emerson and Frost: The Present Act of Vision." *Sewanee Review* 89 (Spring): 206-27.

On Frost's sources of poetic vision in Emerson.

41 PATON, PRISCILLA M. "Robert Frost: 'The fact is the sweetest dream that labor knows.'" *American Literature* 53 (March): 43-55.

On the knowledge of work in "After Apple-Picking," "Mowing," and "Birches." "Frost does not confuse fact and dream for the sake of cleverness but to cherish actual moments and disclose how one comes to knowledge."

42 PERRINE, LAURENCE. "Frost's *New Hampshire*, 1-60." *Explicator* 39 (Spring): 38-39.

Offers some modifications to John F. Lynen's interpretation in *The Pastoral Art of Robert Frost* (1960).

43 ____. "Sound and Sense in Frost." In *Robert Frost: The Man and the Poet*. Edited by Earl J. Wilcox. Winthrop Studies on Major Modern Writers. Rock Hill, S.C.: Winthrop College, pp. 143-56.

Discusses Frost's use of meter as it contributes to meaning in several poems, especially as it portrays "the rhythms and intonations of common speech."

44 ROSS, HAJ. "Robert Frost's 'Out, Out–': A Way In." In *Crossing the Boundaries in Linguistics: Studies Presented to Manfred Bierwisch*. Edited by Wolfgang Klein and Willem Levelt. Dordrecht, Holland: D. Reidel Publishing Co., pp. 265-82.

Analyzes the poem in terms of linguistics, with equations and graphs.

45 ROTELLA, GUY. "Metaphor in Frost's 'The Oven Bird.'" In *Robert Frost: The Man and the Poet*. Edited by Earl J. Wilcox. Winthrop Studies on Major Modern Writers. Rock Hill, S.C.: Winthrop College, pp. 19-30.

Suggests that Frost deliberately lets the metaphor "break down" and "that the poem's implied metaphorical use of the bird as exemplar of and instructor in a strategically reduced poetic is itself based in a Romantic assertion from which the poem, in its last lines, withdraws."

46 SALTER, MARY JO. "Robert Frost: Life with Poetry." *Washington Post Book World*, 13 September, p. 8.

Review of *A Restless Spirit: The Story of Robert Frost*, by Natalie Bober (1981.5). Chides the author for not providing a "wholly honest" account for children of Frost's life, but concludes that the book is useful to introduce children to Frost's poetry.

47 SAUNDERS, JUDITH P. "Frost's 'Once by the Pacific.'" *Explicator* 39 (Summer): 29-31.

Describes the poem's "irreverent humor" as the source of its "ultimate horror."

48 SEARS, JOHN F. "Frost's Figures of Upright Posture." In *Robert Frost: The Man and the Poet*. Edited by Earl J. Wilcox. Winthrop Studies on Major Modern Writers. Rock Hill, S.C.: Winthrop College, pp. 49-59.

Examines one version of Frost's "constant symbol, namely the figure of alertness, skill and poise represented by the woodsplitter, the ax-helve, and the swinger of birches."

49 _____. "Robert Frost and the Imagists: The Background of Frost's 'Sentence Sounds.'" *New England Quarterly* 54 (December): 467-80.

Suggests that Frost's vocabulary and intonations were developed early in order to resist the influence of Imagism.

50 SHARMA, T.R.S. *Robert Frost's Poetic Style*. Atlantic Highlands, N.J.: Humanities Press, 150 pp.

"This study is concerned primarily with Robert Frost's poetry and its stylistic features, that is, the figures of thought such as metonymy, synecdoche, and metaphor and their linguistic correlatives."

51 WADDELL, WILLIAM S., Jr. "By Precept and Example: Aphorism in 'The Star-Splitter.'" In *Robert Frost: The Man and the Poet*. Edited by

1981

Earl J. Wilcox. Winthrop Studies on Major Modern Writers. Rock Hill, S.C.: Winthrop College, pp. 115-24.

Examines the poem in terms of "the New England penchant for aphoristic patterns of speech, for those brief and balanced statements whose very sound and structure suggest confidence and finality."

52 ____. "Figures of the Will: Aphorism in the Poetry of Robert Frost." *DAI* 42, 06A, p. 2679. Ph.D. dissertation, University of North Carolina, Chapel Hill, 226 pp.

"Frost's aphorisms demonstrate his skill as a prosodist through his use of rhythm, parallelism, assonance, and other devices of syntax to give his aphorisms the balance, stability, and integrity that make such statements recognizable by their sound alone."

53 WILCOX, EARL J., ed. *Robert Frost: The Man and the Poet*. Winthrop Studies on Major Modern Writers. Rock Hill, S.C.: Winthrop College, 156 pp.

Contents: Cleanth Brooks, "Frost and Nature"; Guy Rotella, "Metaphor in Frost's 'The Oven Bird'"; George Monteiro, "Goring the Ox: Robert Frost, Robert Francis, and the Intentional Fallacy"; George W. Nitchie, "Frost and the Unwritten Epic"; John F. Sears, "Frost's Figures of Upright Posture"; Donald J. Greiner, "Factual Men and Imagining Rabbits: Robert Frost and Wallace Stevens"; Clifford Lyons, "Walks and Talks with Robert Frost"; Ronald Bieganowski, "*North of Boston*: Human Dimensions to Robert Frost's Spiritual Realm"; Julian Mason, "'Out of the Air': The Friendship of Robert Frost and Lewis Chase"; William S. Waddell, Jr., "By Precept and Example: Aphorism in 'The Star-Splitter'"; Marjorie E. Cook, "Dilemmas of Interpretation: Ambiguities and Practicalities"; Laurence Perrine, "Sound and Sense in Frost." Reissued: 1989.22.

*54 YOSHIMURA, KIYOSHI. "Kyomu to Kodoku: Gendaishijin Toshiteno Robert Frost" [Nihilism and solitude: Robert Frost, a modern poet]. *Chukyo Daigaku Bungakubu Kiyo* (Japan) 16:1-53.

55 YOUNG, HOWARD T. "Lo que dicen los árboles: La amistad literaria entre Robert Frost y Juan Ramón Jiménez." *La Torre* (Universidad de Puerto Rico) 29 (January-December): 289-309.

Describes Frost's friendship with the Spanish poet and translator, who was his Spanish translator as well.

56 ZARANKA, WILLIAM. "Robert Frost's Left-Leaning *Trespassers Will Be Shot* Sign." *Brand-X Anthology of Poetry*. Cambridge, Mass.: Apple-Wood Books, pp. 263-64.

Poem parodying "Mending Wall."

1982

1 ADAMS, STEPHEN J. "Black Cottages: Frost, Eliot, and the Fate of Individualism." *Cithara* 22 (November): 39-52.

Describes the similarities and differences between the two poets, who were not cordial acquaintances.

*2 BARBOUR, LINDA LEE. "Lyric Definition: Poetry as Definitive Play." *American Doctoral Dissertations* (1982) 83-03513. Ph.D. dissertation, University of California, Irvine, 371 pp.

3 BEACH-VITI, ETHEL. "Frost's 'Mowing.'" *Explicator* 40 (Summer): 45-46.

Describes the poem as "about poetry in which the action of the scythe is a metaphor for the composition of the poem."

4 BIEGANOWSKI, RONALD. "Robert Frost's Further Range of the Spirit." *American Benedictine Review* 33 (September): 312-24.

Examines Frost's questionings of experience by which "he discovers patterns in his life, further dimensions to the universe, and he lives with the belief in himself, in his poetry, in the world."

5 ____. "Robert Frost's *New Hampshire*: Realm Not Region." *Literature and Belief*, no. 2, pp. 83-92.

In *New Hampshire* "Frost creates a central poem echoing through the Notes and Grace Notes sections its perception of ultimate dimensions to the universe. Specific locales reveal different aspects of the boundless realm."

6 BROMWICH, DAVID. "Wordsworth, Frost, Stevens, and the Poetic Vocation." *Studies in Romanticism* 21 (Spring): 87-100.

On the treatment of the vocation of poetry in Frost ("Two Tramps in Mud Time"), Stevens ("The Cause of a Particular"), and Wordsworth ("Resolution and Independence"). Reprinted: 1986.6.

7 CLARK, JOHN R. "Frost, Foodstuff, and Verfremdungseffekt." *Notes on Contemporary Literature* 12 (September): 10-12.

On Frost's mix of violent images with those of food and eating, as in "Out, Out–," "The Subverted Flower," and "Design."

8 COLLINS, MICHAEL J. "Poetry and Empiricism: The Example of Three Poems." *CRUX: A Journal on the Teaching of English* (Pretoria, South Africa) 16 (January): 21-27.

On Frost's treatment of empiricism in "The Rose Family" compared to W.H. Auden's in "The Unknown Citizen" and T.S. Eliot's in *Triumphal March*.

9 DANIEL, CHARLES L. "Tonal Contrasts in the Imagery of Robert Frost." *West Georgia College Review* 14 (May): 12-15.

On the light and dark imagery in the poetry.

10 EDWARDS, C. HINES, Jr. "Frost's 'Dust of Snow.'" *Notes on Contemporary Literature* 12 (March): 3-4.

Finds the poem more complicated than other critics do, and suggests that it is about "a cosmic joke" being played on the speaker.

11 EKAMBARAM, E.J. "Primal Concerns in the Poetry of Robert Frost." *Indian Journal of American Studies* 12 (January): 23-32.

Discusses images of human handiwork and survival in several of the poems.

12 FLEISSNER, ROBERT F. "Frost's 'Once by the Pacific.'" *Explicator* 40 (Summer): 46-47.

Reply to 1979.5. Disagrees that the reference to divine "rage" is blasphemous.

13 ____. *That Shakespeherian Rag Again: Frost's Sound of Sense and T.S. Eliot*. Ames: Iowa State University Press, 6 pp.

Deals with T.S. Eliot's fourfold use of "O" and Frost's in unpublished lectures at the New School for Social Research, preserved in the Dartmouth College Library.

14 ____. "Tufting the Host: Frost's Further Use of Wordsworth." *Notes on Contemporary Literature* 12 (September): 6-8.

Describes echoes of Wordsworth's "The Daffodils" in Frost's "The Tuft of Flowers."

15 FRANK, BERNHARD. "Frost's 'Stopping by Woods on a Snowy Evening.'" *Explicator* 40 (Summer): 43-45.

Argues that "there is a before-stopping and there is an after-stopping; but the actual stopping to commune with nature and self never occurs."

*16 FUJIMOTO, MASAKI. "Choshi 'New Hampshire' no Sekai, 1" [The world of "New Hampshire," 1]. *Bungaku to Hyoron* (Japan) 18:46-59.

*17 ____. "Choshi 'New Hampshire' no Sekai, 2" [The world of "New Hampshire," 2]. *Bungaku to Hyoron* (Japan) 19:44-61.

*18 ____. "'Nishi ni Nagareru Kawa' no Sekai, 1: 'Shonen no Kokoro' e" [The world of *West-Running Brook*, 1: From *A Boy's Will* to "An Adult's Will"]. *Osaka Taiiku Daigaku Kiyo* (Japan) 13:93-114.

19 GAGE, JOHN T. "Rhetoric and Dialectic in Robert Frost's *A Masque of Reason*." *Pacific Coast Philology* 17 (November): 82-91.

Finds sources in the Old Testament and Plato for Frost's treatment of reason. The masque expresses a faith in the human faculties to deal adequately with the limits of reason without having to abandon reason or deny it."

20 GERBER, PHILIP L., ed. *Critical Essays on Robert Frost*. Boston: G.K. Hall, 247 pp.

Reprints: Ezra Pound, "*A Boy's Will*" (1913); Ezra Pound, "Modern Georgics" (1914); Amy Lowell, "*North of Boston*" (1915); Sylvester Baxter, "New England's New Poet" (1915); William Stanley Braithwaite, "Robert Frost, New American Poet" (1915); Edward Garnett, "A New American Poet" (1915); Carl Wilmore, "A Visit in Franconia" (1916); [Philadelphia *Public Ledger*], "Of Axe-Handles and Guide-Book Poetry" (1916); Rose C. Feld, "Robert Frost Relieves His Mind" (1923); Anonymous, "Robert Frost" (1924); Percy H. Boynton, "Robert Frost" (1924); Carl Van Doren, "Soil of the Puritans" (1924); Allen Shoenfield, "Science Can't Dishearten Poets, Says Robert Frost" (1925); Elizabeth Shepley Sergeant, "Good Greek out of New England" (1927); Granville Hicks, "The World of Robert Frost" (1930); Horace Gregory, "Robert Frost's New Poems" (1936); Malcolm Cowley, "Frost: A Dissenting Opinion" (1944); Bernard DeVoto, "The Critics and Robert Frost" (1938); Randall Jarrell, "Tenderness and Passive Sadness" (1947); John Mason Potter, "A Visit to 35 Brewster Street" (1952); "Meet the Press" [Freedom and the Poet] (1956); Alvan S. Ryan, "Frost and Emerson: Voice and Vision" (1959); S.P.C. Duvall, "Robert Frost's 'Directive' out of *Walden*" (1960); James M. Cox, "Robert Frost and the Edge of the Clearing" (1959); Roberts W.

French, "Robert Frost and the Darkness of Nature" (1978); William G. O'Donnell, "Robert Frost at Eighty-Eight" (1962); Isadore Traschen, "Robert Frost: Some Divisions in a Whole Man" (1965); Philip L. Gerber, "'My Rising Contemporaries': Robert Frost Amid His Peers" (1966); Arthur M. Sampley, "The Myth and the Quest: The Stature of Robert Frost" (1971); W.W. Robson, "The Achievement of Robert Frost" (1966); Donald J. Greiner, "The Indispensable Robert Frost" (see 1982.23).

21 ____. *Robert Frost*. Twayne's United States Authors Series. Rev. ed. Boston: Twayne Books, 203 pp.

An updated version of the 1966 biographical and critical book.

22 GOWLER, STEVE. "Frost's 'In Hardwood Groves.'" *Explicator* 40 (Spring): 48.

Offers two possible readings of the last two lines of the poem, both expressing "Frost's conviction that the Human horror of non-causality can be symbolically and emotionally transcended through the imaginative reappropriation of the ancient mythological cycle of life, death, and rebirth."

23 GREINER, DONALD J. "The Indispensable Robert Frost." In *Critical Essays on Robert Frost*. Edited by Philip L. Gerber. Boston: G.K. Hall, pp. 220-40.

Chooses twelve items as indispensable: a letter to John T. Bartlett (1914); "Education by Poetry: A Meditative Monologue"; "Letter to *The Amherst Student*"; "Sermon by Robert Frost" (1947); "Storm Fear"; "Home Burial"; "After Apple-Picking"; "An Old Man's Winter Night"; "Stopping by Woods on a Snowy Evening"; "Design"; "The Subverted Flower"; and "Directive." Reprinted in 1982.20.

24 HADAS, RACHEL. "Form, Cycle, Infinity: Landscape Imagery in the Poetry of Robert Frost and George Seferis." *DAI* 42, 11A, p. 4820. Ph.D. dissertation, Princeton University, 306 pp.

Compares Frost and the Greek poet in terms of images: stones (walls), growing things, and stars. Reprinted as book: 1985.12.

25 HÜHN, PETER. "Robert Frost und Edward Thomas: Zur Frage des literarischen Einflusses." In *Die amerikanische Literatur in der Weltliteratur: Themen und Aspekte*. Edited by Claus Uhlig and Volker Bischoff. Berlin: Schmidt, pp. 252-70.

Examines the influence of each poet on the other.

26 IWAYAMA, TAJIRÓ. "Robert Frost." In *America Bungaku no Jikotenkai: 20-seiki no America Bungaku II*. Edited by Toshihiko Ogata. Kyoto: Yamaguchi, pp. 439-75.

Examines Frost's poems that direct attention to life by showing lifeless objects and natural life that is almost dying: "In Hardwood Groves," "October," "My Butterfly," "Spring Pools," and "A Star in a Stone-Boat".

27 KANN, DAVID. "Deadly Serious Play: Robert Frost's 'Design.'" *Hartford Studies in Literature* 14, no. 1:23-32.

Concludes: "Play masters grief; philosophy is play; through play, inner pain is externalized, managed, and thus to some extent relieved."

28 LATHEM, EDWARD CONNERY, and HYDE COX, eds. *Prose Jottings of Robert Frost: Selections from His Notebooks and Miscellaneous Manuscripts*. Lunenberg, Vt.: Northeast-Kingdom Publishers, 145 pp.

Prints selections from notebooks and manuscripts bequeathed by Frost to Kathleen Morrison and presented by her to the Dartmouth College Library.

29 McSWEENEY, KERRY. "Frost's Commentators: The Weak and the Strong." *Critical Quarterly* 24 (Summer): 19-24.

Evaluates recent critics of Frost, finding some "weak" and some "strong." Comments on Pritchard, W.J. Keith, David Perkins, John C. Kemp, and Richard Poirier.

30 MARKS, HERBERT. "The Counter-Intelligence of Robert Frost." *Yale Review* 71 (Summer): 554-78.

On Frost's use of the Bible and Milton's *Paradise Lost* in his treatment of concealment and revelation. Reprinted in: 1986.6.

31 MATTHEWS, WILLIAM. "On the Porch at the Frost Place, Franconia, N.H." *Atlantic Monthly* 249 (February): 51.

Sixty-two line poem in iambic trimeter.

32 MICHAELS, WALTER BENN. "Getting Physical." *Raritan* 2 (Fall): 103-13.

On the poetic voice and dramatic monologue in Frost's poetry. Finds sources in William James's *The Principles of Psychology*.

1982

*33 MIYAKE, TAKUO. "Frost no Shi niokeru 'Ishiki'" [Consciousness in Frost's poems]. *Gaikoku Bungaku Kenkyu* (Nara Joshi Daigaku) (Japan) 4:47-66.

34 MONTEIRO, GEORGE. "'I Always Keep Seeing a Light as I Talk with Him': Limning the Robert Frost/Ridgely Torrence Relationship." *South Carolina Review* 15 (Fall): 32-43.

On Frost's friendship with the editor of the *New Republic* and the influence on some of Frost's poems.

35 MOTION, ANDREW. "Strategies of Discretion." *Times Literary Supplement*, 26 March, p. 333.

Review of *Robert Frost and Sidney Cox: Forty Years of Friendship*, by William R. Evans (1981.13) and Thompson and Lathem, *Robert Frost: Farm-Poultryman* (1963). Writes approvingly of both books and their contributions to understanding Frost and his work.

36 OELSCHLAGER, FRITZ. "Two Woodchucks, or Frost and Thoreau and the Art of the Burrow." *Colby Library Quarterly* 18 (December): 214-19.

On the similarities between Frost's woodchuck and Thoreau's in *Walden*, especially in the significance of burrowing.

37 PERRINE, LAURENCE. "Frost's 'Dust of Snow.'" *Notes on Contemporary Literature* 12 (May): 2-4.

Reply to 1982.10. Finds the poem's idea simple after all.

38 _____. "On Frost's 'The Wood-Pile.'" *Notes on Modern American Literature* 6 (Spring-Summer): Item 1.

Analyzes the structure of the poem as it contributes to meaning.

39 PERRY, JOHN OLIVER. "The Dialog of Voices in Frost." *South Atlantic Quarterly* 81 (Spring): 214-29.

Describes Frost's two voices: the down-to-earth, common-sense pastoral speaker and the behind-the-scenes poet with broader meanings.

40 POIRIER, RICHARD. "Frost, Winnicott, Burke." *Raritan* 2 (Fall): 114-27.

Discusses the influence of Emerson, Kenneth Burke, and D.W. Winnicott, British psychoanalyst. Finds Frost "the Hawthorne of American poetry."

41 RICHMAN, ROBERT. "In Search of Edward Thomas." *New Criterion* 1 (December): 1-16.

Provides biographical information about Frost's closest friend and critical background of his poetry. Concludes that Thomas' reputation has suffered because he "did not have Frost's combative spirit."

42 ROBBINS, J. ALBERT. *An Interlude with Robert Frost: Being a Brief Correspondence with the Poet and Recollections*. Bloomington, Ind.: Private Press of Frederic Brewer, 24 pp.

Interview and three letters by a former University of Florida undergraduate who encouraged Frost to read there in 1938.

43 SABIN, MARGERY. "The Fate of the Frost Speaker." *Raritan* 2 (Fall): 128-39.

Defends examination of "speaking tones" and voice in Frost's poetry against the poststructuralists who "have taken the 'privileging' of speech as a main target for 'demistification.'"

44 St. ARMAND, BARTON LEVI. "Frost's 'Mending Wall.'" *Explicator* 41 (Fall): 47-48.

On the possible influence of Thoreau's *Walden*, originally called "*Walled-in* Pond."

45 SANDERS, CHARLES. "Frost's 'Skeptic.'" *Explicator* 40 (Spring): 47-48.

On the brain as camera-eye in the poem.

46 SCHAKEL, PETER J. "Frost's 'Out, Out–.'" *Explicator* 40 (Summer): 47-48.

Sums up explications of the poem, finding them not incompatible.

47 SUN, CECILE CHU-CHIN. "A Sense of Scene: Depictions of Scene as Expressions of Feeling in Chinese and English Poetry." *DAI* 43, 08A, p. 2660. Ph.D. dissertation, Indiana University, 501 pp.

Deals primarily with Chinese poetry "as expression of feeling," using the notion of *ching* (inner feeling) and ching (outer reality). Mentions Frost as a paradigm for the "immanent" mode.

48 TEFS, WAYNE. "The Faces of Robert Frost." *Canadian Review of American Studies* 13 (Fall): 223-29.

Review of 1981.13, 1979.29, and 1980.28. Writes approvingly of all three.

1982

49 WAHLQUIST, ELIZABETH. "Robert Frost: A Reminiscence." *Literature and Belief*, no. 2, pp. 94-103.

Recalls Frost's readings and talks at the Bread Loaf School of English at Middlebury College in the summers of 1958 through 1962.

50 WILHELM, ALBERT E. "Robert Frost's Proverbial Promises: Indian Responses to 'Stopping by Woods.'" *Motif* 4 (October): 7.

Discusses Frost's use of Indian proverbs.

51 WILL, NORMAN P. "Robert Frost's 'Beech': Faith Regained." *Notes on Modern American Literature* 6 (Spring-Summer): Item 2.

Suggests that the poem is a "cornerstone of *A Witness Tree* as it asserts both technically and thematically the powers and beliefs Frost needed to reaffirm after Elinor's death."

*52 YAMADA, TAKEO. "Robert Frost no Jinbutsu nimirareru Washa to 'Sentence Sound'" [Speaker and "sentence sound" in Robert Frost's character poems]. *Kwansei Gakuin Daigaku Ronko* (Japan) 51:149-69.

1983

*1 ANDO, CHIYOKO. "Robert Frost no Shiniokeru Kodoku no Sekai: 'Desert Places' o Chushinni" [The world of solitude in Robert Frost's poetry: On "Desert Places"]. *Saniku Gakuin Tankidaigaku Kiyo* (Japan) 12:1-20.

2 BIEGANOWSKI, RONALD. "Sense of Time in Robert Frost's Poetics: A Particular Influence of Henri Bergson." *Resources for American Literary Studies* 13 (Autumn): 184-93.

Demonstrates specifically the ways the writings of Henri Bergson influenced Frost's theory of poetry.

3 COLMAN, P.D. "Stylistic Analysis and Literary Criticism, with Specific Reference to Robert Frost's 'Stopping by Woods on a Snowy Evening.'" *CRUX: A Journal on the Teaching of English* (Pretoria, South Africa) 17 (May): 20-30.

Discusses the usefulness and innovations of linguistic study of poetry, using Frost's poem as example. Sees the linguist as "provider of information; evidence for the literary critic" and "as analyzer of the text in isolation as opposed to context."

4 COOK, MARJORIE. "The Serious Play of Interpretation." *South Carolina Review* 15 (Spring): 77-87.

"Because Frost knows our commitments are to our interpretations, our metaphors, he keeps a detachment in an awareness he might be wrong. He knows what he is risking, but he risks – sometimes almost everything."

5 CORDERY, GARETH. "Frost's 'Design.'" *Explicator* 41 (Spring): 45-47.

Reply to Hiatt (*Explicator* 28 [January 1970]). Disagrees that the poem ends on a note of certainty.

6 FANG, PING. "Not Pity But Respect: Humanism Revealed in 'The Death of the Hired Man.'" *Foreign Literature Studies* (People's Republic of China) 20 (June): 6-9.

On human relations in the poem.

7 FARRELL, LEIGH ANN DAWES. "The Archetypal Image: An Interpretation of the Poetry of Theodore Roethke, Arthur Rimbaud, William Butler Yeats, and Robert Frost." *DAI* 44, 11A, p. 3377. Ph.D. dissertation, University of Washington, 245 pp.

Studies of archetypal images in the poets. Frost's "Mending Wall," "An Old Man's Winter Night," and "Directive" reveal "the ambivalent nature of the senex (old man) archetype," in which "lies the symbolic paradigm of the human situation."

8 FRIBERG, INGEGERD. "An Interpretation of Robert Frost's Poem 'After Apple-Picking.'" *Moderna Språk* (Stockholm) 77 (Spring): 325-28.

Interprets the poem as: "The tree is the Tree of Life. The ladder is man's way through life. The fact that the ladder is sticking through the tree and points towards heaven suggests that there is something beyond this life."

*9 FUJIMOTO, MASAKI. "Frost Shi no Onnatachi: 'Meshitsukaitachi no Meshitsukai" [Women in Frost's poems: "A Servant to Servants"]. *Bungaku to Hyoron* (Japan) 20:62-75.

*10 ____. "Poetry and Poetics of Robert Frost." *Osaka Taiiku Daigaku Kiyo* (Japan) 14:77-119.

11 GENTRY, MARSHALL BRUCE. "Five Poems and One: Frost's 'The Hill Wife.'" *CCTE Proceedings* (Conference of College Teachers of English Studies) 48 (September): 110-15.

Discusses the five lyrics individually and in combination to see the structure of the whole and to "understand more fully the husband's point of view and the pathos of his situation."

12 GONZÁLEZ MARTÍN, JERÓNIMO P. "Aproximación a la poesiá de Robert Frost." *Cuadernos Hispanoamericanos: Revista Mensual de Cultura Hispanica* (Madrid) 394 (April): 101-53.

Provides an overview of Frost's life and his books of poetry chronologically, including the masques. Some poems are discussed as to theme and tone.

13 GOZZI, RAYMOND D. "Frost's 'The Gift Outright.'" *Explicator* 41 (Spring): 44-45.

Offers interpretations of the concluding line of the poem.

14 GREENHUT, D.S. "Colder Pastoral: Keats, Frost, and the Transformation of Lyric." *Mid-Hudson Language Studies* no. 6, pp. 49-55.

Compares Frost's landscape to that of Keats. Examines "Never Again Would Birds' Song Be the Same" and "West-Running Brook."

*15 HARADA, ASAKICHI. "'The Subverted Flower': Cro-Magnon-ka sareta Pierrot" ["The Subverted Flower": Pierrot turned into a Cro-Magnon]. *Mukogawa Joshi Daigaku Kiyo, Bungaku Hen* (Japan) 31:1-9.

In English.

*16 ISHIDO, TETSUYA. "Robert Frost to New England: 'A Boy's Will' kara 'New Hampshire' made" [Robert Frost and New England: From "A Boy's Will" to "New Hampshire"]. *Bunka Kiyo* (Hirosaki Daigaku Kyoyobu) (Japan) 17:77-105.

*17 IWASE, SHITSUYU. "Frost niokeru Amarerumono no Image no Oboegaki" [The image of the knitted in Frost: A note]. *Jinbun Kenkyu* (Osaka-shiritsu Daigaku Bungakubu) 35:68-71.

18 JOYCE, JOHN J. "Robert Frost's 'The Witch of Coös': A Matter of Choice." *College Literature* 10 (Spring): 189-93.

Concludes that "man has actual choice when dealing with matters of life and death – and life after death; but his choice has been to deny. A short-sighted, self-defeating choice."

19 KATZ, SANDRA LEE. "The Subverted Flower: The Life of Elinor White Frost and Her Influence on the Poetry of Robert Frost." *DAI* 44, 10A, p. 3066. Ph.D. dissertation, University of Massachusetts, 294 pp.

Examines the biographical evidence and the influence on Frost's poetry. Published as book: 1988:18.

20 KAU, JOSEPH. "Frost's 'Away!': Illusions and Allusions." *Notes on Modern American Literature* 7 (Winter): Item 17.

Suggests that the poem alludes to the folk song, "Shenandoah," and the refrain, "Away! – I'm bound – away."

21 MARKHAM, WAYNE. "Robert Frost's Winter Home For Sale." *Washington Post*, 24 November, Section C, p. 4.

Describes the availability of Frost's South Miami winter residence, designated as a historic site by the city of Miami, with an asking price of $295,000.

22 MARRE, K.E. "Some Uses of Irony in Robert Frost's Poetry." *University of Dayton Review* 16 (Winter): 83-88.

Describes types of irony in the poems. Finds it "a technical resource with which to represent a given speaker's resourcefulness in converting experience into memorable statement."

*23 MIYAKE, TAKUO. "Frost no Shi niokeru 'Ishiki'" [Consciousness in Frost's poems]. *Gaikoku Bungaku Kenkyu* (Nara Joshi Daigaku) (Japan) 5:77-105.

24 MONTEIRO, GEORGE. "A Way *Out* of Something': Robert Frost's Emily Dickinson." *Centennial Review* 27 (Summer): 192-203.

On Frost's familiarity with Dickinson's poetry. Comments also on Louise Bogan, Archibald MacLeish, and Richard Wilbur. Also provides an imaginary "talk" by Frost on Dickinson, in the Frost manner.

*25 NARITA, MICHIKO. "Robert Frost Ko, 6: 'New Hampshire,' Jojoshi no Fukken" [A study of Robert Frost, 6: "New Hampshire," revival of lyrics]. *Jissen Eibungaku* (Japan) 23:74-82.

26 OELSCHLAGER, FRITZ. "Robert Frost's 'The Pasture': A Reconsideration." *Concerning Poetry* 16 (Fall): 1-9.

Examines the poem's tone and Frost's relationship to the pastoral tradition.

1983

27 ORR, ED. "The Road Once Taken." In *A Tribute to Daniel Smythe*. Edited by Dennis Q. McInerny. Peoria, Ill.: Bradley University, pp. 54-58.

Provides a recollection of Smythe, poet and professor at Bradley, who had published often on Frost and was an admirer.

28 PERRINE, LAURENCE. "Frost's 'Nothing Gold Can Stay.'" *Explicator* 42 (Fall): 38-39.

Describes the botanical language of the poem and suggests possible meanings.

29 ____. "Frost's 'Once by the Pacific.'" *Explicator* 41 (Spring): 44.

Reply to 1981.10. Finds nothing humorous in Frost's descriptions. "In Frost's picture the great waves 'coming in' are all looking in one direction – toward shore, not at each other."

30 ____. "Frost's 'Revelation.'" *Explicator* 42 (Fall): 36-38.

Reply to Bassett (*Explicator* 3 [1945], p. 42). Finds his discussion "a total miscomprehension of the poem."

31 ____. "Frost's 'The Tuft of Flowers.'" *Explicator* 42 (Fall): 36.

Reply to Bassett (*Explicator* 3 [1945], p. 42). Finds his argument "unsupportable."

32 ____. "Robert Frost's 'The Hill Wife': Evidence, Inference, and Speculation in the Interpretation of Poetry." *College Literature* 10 (Winter): 1-15.

Analyzes the five sections of the poem and illustrates "the process of knowing, inferring, and speculating by addressing specific questions to the poem," eight in all.

33 RUDERMAN, JUDITH. "Milton's Choices: Styron's Use of Robert Frost's Poetry in *Lie Down in Darkness*." *College Language Association Journal* 27 (December): 141-51.

Suggests that in spite of William Styron's distaste for Frost's poetry, his references to poems in his novel complement his themes and show "a clear kinship between the value systems of the two writers."

34 SCHEVILL, JAMES. "At Frost's Farm in Derry, New Hampshire." In *The American Fantasies: Collected Poems 1945-1987*. Chicago: Swallow Press, p. 177.

Twenty-two-line poem that recalls Frost's artistic influence.

1983

35 SEARS, JOHN F. "The Subversive Performer in Frost's 'Snow' and 'Out, Out–.'" In *The Motive for Metaphor: Essays in Modern Poetry*. Edited by Francis C. Blessington and Guy Rotella. Boston: Northeastern University Press, pp. 82-92.

On Frost's imaginative playing with realistic settings and characters. Frost performs as an actor by implication.

36 SELL, ROGER D. "Three Separate Leaves from Robert Frost's Derry Years: A Note and Transcriptions." *Studies in Bibliography* 36:229-32.

Describes notes in Frost's handwriting in the Clifton Waller Barrett Collection at the University of Virginia Library.

37 SHEEHY, DONALD G. "Robert Frost and 'The Lockless Door.'" *New England Quarterly* 56 (March): 39-59.

Discusses Frost's *A Way Out*, "The Lockless Door," and *The Guardeen* as they "demonstrate the crucial tension in Frost between solitude and community as well as his shifting perspective on the role of the artist in society."

38 SLIGHTS, WILLIAM W.E. "The Sense of Frost's Humor." *Concerning Poetry* 16 (Spring): 29-42.

Discusses Frost's humor in theory and in practice.

39 SUTTON, WILLIAM A. "Some Robert Frost 'Fooling.'" *Mark Twain Journal* 21 (Spring): 61-62.

Describes some aspects of Frost's relationship with the Mark Twain Society. Includes comments on Cyril Clemens' *A Chat with Robert Frost* (1940).

40 TRIKHA, MANORAMA B. *Robert Frost: Poetry of Clarifications*. Atlantic Highlands, N.J.: Humanities Press, 259 pp.

"As Frost's thoughts attained new dimensions they conglomerated into a vision which offers 'clarifications' for the soul and body scars and finally leads towards the source."

41 WADDELL, WILLIAM S., Jr. "Robert Frost's 'Home Burial': A Drama of Tradition and Memory." *Perspectives on Contemporary Literature*, no. 9, pp. 76-82.

Discusses "the tension between self and society" presented "through tradition and memory" in the poem.

42 WAKEFIELD, RICHARD PAUL. "Robert Frost and the Opposing Lights of the Hour." *DAI* 44, 04A, p. 1089. Ph.D. dissertation, University of Washington, 231 pp.

Examines three main themes in the poetry: "the relationship between self and nature, the relationship between self and society, and the effect of romantic love on the sense of individuality." Reprinted as book: 1985.25.

43 WHITLOCK, BAIRD W. "Conversations with Robert Frost (from a Work-in-Progress)." *Xavier Review* (New Orleans) n.s. 3, no. 2:1-16.

Reminiscence of Frost at Middlebury College and other places through the years. Recalls discussions of poetry and history, and provides personal anecdotes.

*44 WORDELL, CHARLES B. "Robert Frost from *A Boy's Will* to *North of Boston*." *Chu – Shikoku America Bungakkai* (Japan) 19:1-13.

45 ZUBIZARRETA, JOHN. "Frost, Eliot, and Modernism." *DAI* 45, 01A, p. 181. Ph.D. dissertation, University of South Carolina, 181 pp.

Sees modernist similarities in the two poets. "Eliot is the master of modernism, but Frost is also an influential and vital member of the modernist period."

1984

1 BIEGANOWSKI, RONALD. "Robert Frost's Sense of Choice in *Mountain Interval*." *College Literature* 11 (Fall): 258-68.

Discusses Frost's theme of choosing in terms of William James's theory of choices.

2 CLARKE, PETER B. "Frost's 'Mending Wall.'" *Explicator* 43 (Fall): 48-50.

Describes the poem as illustrating aspects of Roman religious ritual.

3 DIERKES, HENRY. *Robert Frost: A Friend to a Younger Poet.* Introduction by Milton Hindus. Notasulga, Ala.: Armstrong Press, 77 pp.

Describes literary correspondence begun in 1934 and Frost's encouragement to a beginning poet. Contains facsimiles of Frost autographs.

4 EDMUNDS, PAUL. "Study-Aids: Help or Hindrance? Two Poems about Affliction." *CRUX: A Journal on the Teaching of English* (Pretoria, South Africa) 18 (January): 38-42.

Uses Milton's "On His Blindness" and Frost's "Out, Out–" to illustrate possibilities for classroom discussion. Criticizes a "study aid" prescribed for students for failing to deal with the poems sensitively and adequately.

5 FANG, PING. "The Translation of a Little Poem." *Foreign Literature Studies* (People's Republic of China) 24 (June): 64.

Comments by a veteran Chinese translator, referring to "The Pasture."

6 FLEISSNER, ROBERT F. "Frost's Ancient Music." *Paideuma* 13 (Winter): 415-17.

Provides a gloss for Frost's "the whole G– d– Machinery" in "Lucretius versus the Lake Poets."

7 ____. "Markin' the Frost Line: On Robert Frost and Edwin Markham." *South Carolina Review* 16 (Spring): 120-24.

Describes parallels between certain poems of Markham and some of Frost's.

8 ____ "Sub Rosa: Frost's 'Five-Petaled' Flower." *Colby Library Quarterly* 20 (December): 206-24.

Discusses the numerological significance of "five" in the poem; however, "it will not do to claim Frost as a literary numerologist *per se*. He was not concerned with such an arcane stance. The bearing of the petal upon several of his poems ... relates rather to a classical formulation (only by derivation Pythagorean) of the Golden Mean Proportion alone." Reprinted in 1989.6.

*9 FRAZIER, JOHN. "Robert Frost: Sage or Spiritual Drifter?" *Bulletin of Sakura no Seibo Junior College* (Japan) 9:1-17.

10 GULLACE, GINA. "Intense Fragility: Studies in Lyric." *DAI* 45, 06A, p. 1759. Ph.D. dissertation, State University of New York, Binghamton, 253 pp.

Uses a theory of lyric by Sigurd Burckhardt to examine English and American lyrics, including Frost's "Design."

1984

*11 HABARA, YUKIO. "Robert Frost no Shi: Yakushi to Hyoshaku, 1" [Robert Frost's poetry: Translation and interpretation, 1]. *Joshi Daigaku Kenkyu Kiyo* (Japan) 5:37-56.

12 HALL, DOROTHY JUDD. *Robert Frost: Contours of Belief*. Introduction by Lesley Frost. Athens: Ohio University Press, 148 pp.

Explores Frost's poetry as a "sacred" activity in light of his Puritan heritage, in the poetry, prose, letters, and talks. Reprinted from dissertation: 1973.11.

*13 HARADA, ASAKICHI. "'A Star in a Stone-Boat': Makuro to Mikuro no Ketsugo" ["A Star in a Stone-Boat": Integration of macro and micro]. *Mukogawa Joshi Daigaku Kiyo, Bungakubu Hen* (Japan) 32:1-10.

In English.

14 HARMON, WILLIAM. "Odd Man In." *Parnassus* 12 (Fall-Winter): 72-77.

Review of *Frost: A Literary Life Reconsidered*, by William H. Pritchard (1984.33). Sees the book as "a graceful act of rectification" of Lawrance Thompson's biographical studies.

15 HART, THOMAS ELWOOD. "Frost's 'The Road Not Taken': Text-Structure and Poetic Theory." *Language and Style: An International Journal* 17 (Winter): 3-43.

Uses linguistic science to analyze the form of the poem.

16 HOLLAND, NORMAN N. "The Brain of Robert Frost." *New Literary History* 15 (Winter): 365-85.

On the role of identity in interpretation and the creative process. Concludes: "Creation and interpretation are so akin that creation is a natural metaphor for interpretation." Reprinted: 1988.15.

17 HUZZARD, JERE K. "Frost's 'Design.'" *Explicator* 42 (Summer): 26-28.

Reply to Hiatt (*Explicator* 28 [1970]: Item 41), and Cordery (1983.5). In their discussions they have missed Frost's deliberate ambiguity.

18 KILLINGSWORTH, PAULA. "Four Dimensions of the Isolation Theme in Frost's Poetry." *Publications of the Mississippi Philological Association* 3 (Summer): 1-13.

Sees four kinds of isolation in Frost's poetry: the American Adam overcoming conflicts, self-imposed isolation, emotional entrapment, and the isolated "explorer" in an unfamiliar world.

*19 KOMAMURA, TOSHIO. *Robert Frost no Bokka* [Pastorals of Robert Frost]. Tokyo: Kokubun-sha, 326 pp.

20 MARCUS, MORDECAI. "The Best of Robert Frost: Some Problems of Subjectivity." *Journal of Evolutionary Psychology* 5 (August): 255-62.

Evaluates selections of Frost's poems in anthologies, based on subjective opinions. Chooses "After Apple-Picking," "The Onset," and "An Old Man's Winter Night" as "at the pinnacle of his achievement."

21 MILLER, LEWIS H., Jr. "On Keeping Watch: Robert Frost and Marianne Moore." *College Language Association Journal* 27 (June): 411-18.

On poetic voice and Frost's "Neither Out Far Nor In Deep" compared to Moore's "A Grave."

*22 NAKAUCHI, MASAO. "Robert Frost as a Self-Seeker." *Eigo Eibungaku Kenkyu* (Soka Daigaku) (Japan) 15:1-9.

23 NITCHIE, GEORGE W. Review of *Robert Frost: Contours of Belief*, by Dorothy Judd Hall. *New England Quarterly* 57 (December): 611-13.

See 1984.12. The book "offers not an articulation but an adumbration, recognizing that adumbrations, brilliant as they sometimes were, were mostly what Frost had to offer on the subject."

24 OELSCHLAGER, FRITZ. "The Consecration of Home: Robert Frost's 'The Death of the Hired Man.'" *Essays in Literature* (Macomb, Ill.) 11 (Spring): 105-12.

Adds a third definition of *home* to Frost's two: "Home is the place one comes round to at last, the final resting place in the earth itself."

25 ____. "Fences Make Neighbors: Process, Identity, and Ego in Robert Frost's 'Mending Wall.'" *Arizona Quarterly* 40 (Autumn): 242-54.

On Frost's treatment of the egoism of the speaker and his relationship to his neighbor.

26 OXENHORN, HARVEY. "Water Music: Wordsworth, MacDiarmid, and Frost." *Southern Review* 20 (April): 265-78.

Discusses primarily the poetry of Hugh MacDiarmid (pen name for Christopher Murray Grieve) and the influence of Wordsworth. Some mention of Frost for the sake of comparison.

27 PERRI, CARMELA. "Knowing and Playing: The Literary Text and the Trope Allusion." *American Imago* 41 (Summer): 117-28.

Discusses "Never Again Would Birds' Song Be the Same" to illustrate metalepsis, a kind of literary revisionism that "reveals the way we individuate that self, the figure that has been described as the echo of belatedness which is also the trope of relatedness."

28 PERRINE, LAURENCE. "Frost's 'Design.'" *Explicator* 42 (Winter): 16.

Reply to Bassett (*Explicator* 3 [1945], p. 42). Finds his discussion "almost totally confused."

29 ____. "Frost's 'The Fear': Unfinished Sentences, Unanswered Questions." *College Literature* 11 (Spring): 125-33.

Describes the role of inference in interpretation, and four sources of mystery in the poem.

30 ____. "Robert Frost's 'Provide, Provide.'" *Notes on Modern American Literature* 8 (Spring-Summer): Item 5.

Argues that "the two *recommendations* in the poem are both ironical (the poet does not want us to accept them; he does not even offer the first as a valid choice). The quiet, almost parenthetical *observation*, on the other hand, is really his recommendation."

31 POPOV, IGOR. "The Last Toast of Robert Frost." *Soviet Literature*, 7, no. 436, pp. 136-40.

On Frost's relationship with Soviet writers Konstantin Simonov and Eduardas Miezelaitis, 1960-1963, after their first meeting in Boston in the winter of 1960.

32 PRITCHARD, WILLIAM H. "Deeper Into Life: Robert Frost's Last Years." *American Scholar* 53 (Autumn): 522-32.

Adapted from 1984.33.

33 ____. *Frost: A Literary Life Reconsidered*. New York: Oxford University Press, 286 pp.

In large part a refutation of Lawrance Thompson's three-volume biography. Suggests that Frost's behavior, like his poetry, was a form of "play," by which he sought to educate by witty disruption and shock.

34 THOMAS, JEFFREY CRAWFORD. "The Contextualist Metaphysic of American Modernist Poetry: William James's Influence on Robert Frost, William Carlos Williams, Wallace Stevens & Co." *DAI* 45, 01A, p. 186. Ph.D. dissertation, Ohio State University, 363 pp.

Puts Frost in the modern group, including T.S. Eliot and Ezra Pound.

35 TOMLINSON, SANDRA W. "Frost's 'The Draft Horse.'" *Explicator* 42 (Summer): 28-29.

Describes the people in the poem as "like the absurd heroes of Camus and Beckett."

36 WADDELL, WILLIAM S., Jr. "A Dialectic of Marriage in Robert Frost's Dramatic Poems." In *Portraits of Marriage in Literature*. Edited by Anne C. Hargrove and Maurine Magliocco. Macomb, Ill.: *Essays in Literature*, pp. 125-39.

Applies the theories of Jean-Paul Sartre to the poem. Suggests that in the poems men use broad categories of language, while women use a personal language, resulting in failed communication and misunderstanding. Yet marriage is "an absence, an agency of mutual help and support that may prove stronger than the individual alone in the struggle against the world at large."

37 WALLACE, PATRICIA. "Separateness and Solitude in Frost." *Kenyon Review* n.s. 6 (Winter): 1-12.

Describes solitude and separateness as found in "Mending Wall," as it "confirms our unearned assumptions of togetherness."

38 WILCOX, EARL J. "Psyching-out the Public and His Contemporaries." *McNeese Review* 31 (1984-86): 3-13.

Describes Frost's methods to "manipulate his contemporaries during his rise to fame." Examines Frost's methods in promoting his public image, which was often quite different in reality.

*39 YAMADA, TAKEO. "Robert Frost no Jijoshi to 'Sentence Sound' no Riron" [Robert Frost's lyrics and the theory of "sentence sound"]. *Kwansei Gakuin Daigaku Eibei Bungaku* (Japan) 29:62-78.

*40 YAMAKAWA, GAKUJI. "Frost Shi Kenkyu: Shizen tono Taiwa No Motif" [Frost's motif of dialogue with nature]. *Bunka Kiyo* (Hirosaki Daigaku Kyoyobu) (Japan) 20:7-17.

1984

*41 YOSHIMURA, KIYOSHI. "Robert Frost niokeru Chuyo no Seishin, 1" [Moderation in Robert Frost, 1]. *Chukyo Eibangaku* (Chukyo Daigaku) (Japan) 4:25-48.

1985

1 BARTINI, ARNOLD G. "Whiteness in Robert Frost's Poetry." *Massachusetts Review* 26 (Summer-Autumn): 351-56.

"Whiteness to Frost . . . is inscrutable mystery and passionless Being, tamed by metaphor. It is akin to Eliot's whimper, and never resounds with Melville's roar."

2 BELL, VEREEN. "Robert Frost and the Nature of Narrative." *New England Review and Bread Loaf Quarterly* 8 (Autumn): 70-78.

On Frost's narrative poetry as "the form-making activity of the mind . . . to do justice both to the claims of passing time in the world and to claims of the ordering mind."

3 BLUMENTHAL, JOSEPH. "One Printer and Robert Frost." *American Book Collector* n.s. 6 (March-April): 3-11.

Describes the printing by Spiral Press of limited editions of *The Collected Poems* (1930), *A Boy's Will* (1935), Marjorie Frost Fraser's *Franconia* (1936), and *A Further Range* (1936).

4 ____. *Robert Frost and His Printers*. Austin, Tex.: W. Thomas Taylor, 105 pp.

An interpretive description of limited editions and other special printings of works by Frost, with facsimile reproductions.

5 CLAASEN, JO-MARIE. "Robert Frost's 'Build Soil': A Modern Text Based on an Ancient Mode, the Pastoral." *Theoria* (University of Natal, South Africa) 65 (October): 1-13.

Sees the poem as a Virgilian pastoral, but also examines the political (1930) implications. The "soil-building" metaphor "means: the ploughing in of ideas, like the ploughing in of a crop, will enrich the 'soil' of thought, and in due time will produce a better crop."

6 CLAMPITT, AMY. "The Better Half of Poetry." *Grand Street* 4 (Summer): 155-66.

Prints a paper read on 9 August 1985, at the Frost Place, Franconia, N.H. Describes Frost's use of language and metrics.

7 COOKE, MICHAEL G. "Frost's Poetry: Breaking the Boundaries of the Hidden and the Silent." *Kentucky Review* 5 (Fall): 46-59.

On Frost's treatment of solipsism and silence. Finds sources in the English romantic poets.

8 DIETRICH, R.F. "The Contrary Mr. Frost of 'West-Running Brook.'" *University of Dayton Review* 17 (Winter 1985-86): 83-89.

Sees "Frost struggling to believe in the essential rightness of life's directions, however contrary things looked in the particularity of existence."

9 EDWARDS, C. HINES, Jr. "The Clock in Frost's 'Acquainted with the Night.'" *Notes on Contemporary Literature* 15 (May): 8-9.

Argues that "whatever its symbolic import, the clock must first be a mechanical item observable in the landscape."

10 FRANCIS, LESLEY LEE. "Robert Frost and Susan Hayes Ward." *Massachusetts Review* 26 (Summer-Autumn): 341-50.

Describes Frost's correspondence with the literary editor of the *New York Independent*, which published "My Butterfly" in 1894. Shows the importance of Ward's influence and the bond between the two families that followed.

*11 HABARA, YUKIO. "Robert Frost no Shi: Yakushi to Hyoshaku, 2" [Robert Frost's poetry: Translation and interpretation, 2]. *Kagoshima Joshi Daigaku Kenkyu Kiyo* (Japan) 6:29-52.

12 HADAS, RACHEL. *Form, Cycle, Infinity: Landscape Imagery in the Poetry of Robert Frost and George Seferis*. Lewisburg, Pa.: Bucknell University Press, 221 pp.

Finds parallels in the two poets, although their backgrounds are divergent and they did not know each other's work.

Reprinted from: 1982.24.

13 HADDIN, THEODORE. "Surfaces and Depths: The Metonymic Wells of Thoreau and Frost." *Publications of the Mississippi Philological Association* 4 (Summer): 40-49.

Notes that Thoreau often called Walden Pond a well, then examines the image and its ramifications and their influence on Frost's "For Once, Then, Something."

14 HEATH, WILLIAM. "Robert Frost: Faith and Art." *Canadian Review of American Studies* 16 (Fall): 345-51.

Discusses 1982.23, 1982.28, and 1984.12. Finds Hall's book "welcome," Donald Greiner's article in Gerber's book "indispensable," and Lathem and Cox's "for the aficionado."

15 KENNEDY, X.J. "Robert Frost Discovers Another Road Not Taken." *Cross Ties*. Athens: University of Georgia Press, p. 69.

Twelve-line light verse poem.

16 LAKRITZ, ANDREW MORRIS. "Lyric and Its Times: Frost's and Stevens' Poetry of the Thirties." *DAI*, 46, 04A, p. 983. Ph.D. dissertation, University of California, Irvine, 358 pp.

Reads the lyric poems in a social and political context. "To study the poem is to study the will to power of historical individuals, in constant struggle with contradictory ideologies and social pressures that are both inimical to the poetic enterprise and that make such thinking possible and necessary."

17 LUSIGNAN, NANCY ANNE. "They Cannot Choose But Hear: Auditors in Modern Literary Tradition." *DAI* 46, 03A, p. 708. Ph.D. dissertation, Boston College, 83 pp.

Examines the "audience-focused" nature of poetry since Coleridge's "The Rime of the Ancient Mariner." Sees Frost's "Directive" as akin to Wordsworth's "Tintern Abbey."

18 McGUIRE, JERRY. "The Discourse of the Two Cheeks: Robert Frost's Concept of 'Colloquiality.'" *American Poetry* 2 (Spring): 34-50.

Examines "the question of what it means for a self to be 'embedded inchoately in oral response,' for it is in the *summoning of response* that the poem annihilates any supposed self-boundaries that might be claimed for it."

19 MATTHEWS, WILLIAM. "On the Porch at the Frost Place, Franconia, N.H." In *The Morrow Anthology of Younger American Poets*. Edited by Dave Smith and David Bottoms. New York: Quill, pp. 451-52.

A sixty-two-line poem in approximate iambic tetrameter.

20 PERRINE, LAURENCE. "Misreadings of Frost's 'The Silken Tent.'" *Notes on Modern American Literature* 9 (Spring-Summer): Item 3.

Describes published interpretations as "misreadings" and argues that "capriciousness" describes the tent, not the woman, in the poem.

21 RAABE, DAVID M. "Strategies in Scanning Robert Frost's Poetry with SNOBOL." *Proceedings of the 1985 International Conference on English Language and Literature. Applications of SNOBOL and SPITBOL*. Edited by Eric Johnson. Madison, S.D.: Dakota State College, pp. 132-43.

Uses SNOBOL (*S*tri*N*g *O*riented Sym*BO*lic *L*anguage) to describe computer scansion in Frost's poetry. Finds the meter increasingly less strict in the later works.

22 SELL, ROGER D. "Robert Frost's Plays." *Massachusetts Review* 26 (Summer-Autumn): 265-92.

Introduction to Frost plays, "In an Art Factory" and "The Guardeen," both printed from manuscript, pp. 293-340. Introduction reprinted, revised, from *Robert Frost: Four Studies* (Acta Academiae Aboensis, Series A: *Humaniora*, 57, no. 2, Abo, 1980).

23 SHEEHY, DONALD G. *New England Quarterly* 58 (June): 320-23.

Review of 1984.33. The biography "is a welcome corrective to Thompson's overly harsh view, subtle and elegant in its articulation of Frost's sensibility, it restores the poetry to the life."

24 SUTTON, BETTY S. "Form as Argument: Frost's 'Lesson for Today.'" *Fu Jen Studies: Literature and Linguistics* (Taipei, Taiwan), no. 18, pp. 81-96.

Sees the poem as in the Horatian vernacular mode, with parallels to the ninth-century Alcuin's epitaph in Carolingian Latin.

25 WAKEFIELD, RICHARD. *Robert Frost and the Opposing Lights of the Hour*. New York: Peter Lang, 222 pp.

Describes Frost's purpose as confronting "constraints, but within those constraints we make possibilities. For Frost, the purpose of poetry is the same as the purpose of life: to explore and define the area in which we make ourselves. The opposing lights of the hour are the contradictory circumstances which cast our shadows now this way, now that, allowing us to see ourselves less as we are than as the light happens to catch us. To accept this as the sum of our self-knowledge is to slip into a twilight of indeterminism." Reprinted from: 1983.42.

26 ZACHARASIEWICZ, WALDEMAR. "Die moderne amerikanische Naturdichtung und die pastorale Tradition: Robert Frost." In *Englische und amerikanische Naturdichtung im 20. Jahrhundert*. Edited by Günter Ahrends and Hans Ulrich Seeber. Tübingen: Gunter Narr Verlag, pp. 260-77.

1985

Discusses Frost's poetry in the pastoral tradition, with reference to John Greenleaf Whittier, Wallace Stevens, and William Carlos Williams.

1986

1 ABEL, DARREL. "Robert Frost's 'Range-Finding.'" *Colby Library Quarterly* 22 (December): 225-37.

The poem "considers the discords and overlapping limits between human nature and other parts of living nature inhabiting the same zones that are indifferent to human designs and limits." Discusses several other poems as well.

2 BAGBY, GEORGE F., Jr. "Frost's Synecdochism." *American Literature* 58 (October): 379-92.

Sees the literary device also as providing ways of thinking, of using language, and as devices of symbolism.

3 BELL, BARBARA CURRIER. "Frost on Humanity in Nature." *Arizona Quarterly* 42 (Autumn): 223-38.

Discusses the relation between the human and natural worlds in the poetry generally and the human qualities of nature as the "ruling theme" of Frost's nature poetry.

4 BERGER, CHARLES. "Echoing Eden: Frost and Origins." In *Robert Frost: Modern Critical Views*. Edited by Harold Bloom. New York: Chelsea House Publishers, pp. 147-65.

Suggests that Frost "is a poet of echo rather than allusion." Discusses "origins and echoes" in "The Aim Was Song," "Sitting by a Bush in Broad Sunlight," "A Winter Eden," "The Most of It," and "Directive."

5 BLOOM, HAROLD. Introduction to *Robert Frost: Modern Critical Views*. New York: Chelsea House Publishers, pp. 1-7.

Provides a brief overview of Frost's poetry, some of his Emersonian qualities, and his irony and humor.

6 ____, ed. *Robert Frost: Modern Critical Views*. New York: Chelsea House Publishers, 183 pp.

Contents: Robert Pack, "Frost's Enigmatical Reserve: The Poet as Teacher and Preacher"; Frank Lentricchia, "The Redemptive Imagination"; Richard Poirier, "Choices"; Marie Borroff, "Robert Frost's New Testament: The Uses of Simplicity"; Sydney Lea, "From

Sublime to Rigamarole: Relations of Frost to Wordsworth"; David Bromwich, "Wordsworth, Frost, Stevens and the Poetic Vocation"; Herbert Marks, "The Counter Intelligence of Robert Frost"; Charles Berger, "Echoing Eden: Frost and Origins."

7 BOCK, MARTIN. "Frost's 'The Oven Bird' and the Modern Poetic Idiom." *Texas Review* 7 (Spring-Summer): 28-31.

Interprets the poem as on the traditional idea of metaphorical association of the bird and the poet.

8 BRADFORD, M.E. "Artists at Home: Frost and Faulkner." *Modern Age* 30 (Summer-Fall): 274-82.

"Using the careers of Robert Frost and William Faulkner, with James Joyce set over against them as foil and archetypal modern, I will attempt to replicate the ground for this insight to awakening, to construct a correlative overlay, a better-colored glass through which to read their characteristic works; and to foster with it a notion of American complexity."

9 BURNSHAW, STANLEY. *Robert Frost Himself*. New York: George Braziller, 342 pp.

An attempt to correct Lawrance Thompson's biography with a more sympathetic evaluation of the poet's life. Frost had said: "I'm counting on you to protect me from Larry. Remember."

10 COAKLEY, JOHN. "T.S. Eliot's 'Mr. Apollinax' and Frost's 'The Demiurge's Laugh.'" *Explicator* 45 (Fall): 42-45.

Compares the demonic element in the two poems.

11 COX, JAMES M. "Recovering Frost's Literary Life." *Sewanee Review* 94 (Winter): 118-23.

Review of *Frost: A Literary Life Reconsidered*, by William H. Pritchard (1984.33). Appraises the book with admiration and sensitivity: "As long as Lawrance Thompson's life of Frost remains the standard biography–this book by William Pritchard is indispensable for anyone who would know the full life of Robert Frost."

12 DONALDSON, SCOTT. "Frost, Dickinson, and the Strategy of Evasion." *Concerning Poetry* 19:107-16.

On Frost's knowledge of Dickinson's poetry and similarities of methods of concealment in their work.

1986

13 FLEISSNER, ROBERT F. *The Prince and the Professor: The Wittenberg Connection in Marlowe, Shakespeare, Goethe, and Frost (a Hamlet-Faust[us] Analogy)*. Heidelberg: Carl Winter, 217 pp.

On *Hamlet, Faust, Faustus*, the Book of Job, and "A Masque of Reason."

14 ____. "Retaking 'The Road Not Taken.'" *Notes on Contemporary Literature* 16 (March): 2-5.

Sees the poem as a subliminal parody of poems by Edward Thomas and William Wordsworth.

15 FRANCIS, LESLEY LEE. "A Decade of Stirring Times: Robert Frost and Amy Lowell." *New England Quarterly* 59 (December): 508-22.

Suggests that, although impatient with Lowell's histrionics, Frost respected her as a leader in the rebellion against romanticism and the poetry of the previous generation.

16 GERBER, PHILIP L. "Frost the Man, Frost the Believer." *Contemporary Literature* 27 (Spring): 134-37.

Review article on *Frost: A Literary Life Reconsidered*, by William H. Pritchard, and *Robert Frost: Contours of Belief*, by Dorothy Judd Hall (1984.33 and 1984.12). Disagrees with Pritchard that Frost suffered "no decline" in his later books, but finds areas of the biography "masterful." Says Hall's book is "as thorough a case as might be made" on Frost and "the God question."

17 ____. "Remembering Robert Frost: An Interview with William Jewell." *New England Quarterly* 59 (March): 1-27.

Jewell's parents attended high school with Frost in Lawrence, Mass.

18 INGEBRETSEN, EDWARD JOSEPH. "From Innocence to Experience–Making the Final Unity: The Spiritual Dimension of Robert Frost's Poetry." *DAI* 47, 08A, p. 3038. Ph.D. dissertation, Duke University, 329 pp.

Examines "how Frost's contrasting images–innocence versus experience, being lost or being found, having a home or not having one–address his concern with the 'ultimate'–the spiritual difference that human purpose, love, and intention, makes in the universe."

19 KENNY, DOROTHEA. "Whose Woods?" *Journal of Evolutionary Psychology* 7 (August): 227-40.

Sees the woods as archetypal: "(1) place, or means of entry to the otherworld; (2) location of the divine, especially of the Mother; (3) oracular manifestation of divine providence; (4) place of birth or of rebirth."

20 McPHILLIPS, ROBERT T. "Diverging and Converging Paths: Horizontal and Vertical Movement in Robert Frost's *Mountain Interval*." *American Literature* 58 (March): 82-98.

On kinds of choosing in the poems and the freedom of movement, whereby the poet can "become uprooted, lose the distinction between height and breadth which is the distinguishing characteristic of the strong poet."

21 MOORE, M. SHAWN. "Robert Frost's 'The Pasture': Poem and Metapoem." *Virginia English Bulletin* 36 (Winter): 49-51.

Suggests that the poem "paradoxically discusses poetry at the same time that it is poetry," like a poem on a Möbius strip, a one-sided piece of paper, thus endlessly repeating the same thing.

22 O'BRIEN, TIMOTHY D. "Archetypal Encounter in 'Mending Wall.'" *American Notes and Queries* 24 (May-June): 147-51.

Discusses the poem in light of Jung's theory of personal psychology.

23 OELSCHLAGER, FRITZ. "West Toward Heaven: The Adventure of Metaphor in Robert Frost's 'West-Running Brook.'" *Colby Library Quarterly* 22 (December): 238-51.

Discusses the influence of Emerson, William James, and Henri Bergson on the poem.

24 ORLOV, PAUL A. "The World's Disorder and the Word's Design in Two Poems by Frost." *Journal of the Midwest Language Association* 19 (Fall): 30-38.

Attempts to show how "Frost poetically transcends nihilism" in "Design" and "Desert Places."

25 PEAN, JAMES LOUIS. "Snow in Frost." *DAI* 46, 03A, p. 2694. Ph.D. dissertation, St. John's University, 156 pp.

Sees snow as an expression of self-discovery, as "a means of both 'terrifying' and 'inspiring' his readers through paradox," as a unifying motif, and as "symbolic shorthand" to illustrate the problems of imagination.

1986

26 ROGERS, WILLIAM E. "Mysteries in Frost." *Furman Studies* 32 (December): 53-64.

Uses Roman Jakobson's analysis of communicative situation to discuss "For Once, Then, Something."

27 SHAW, W. DAVID. "The Poetics of Pragmatism: Robert Frost and William James." *New England Quarterly* 59 (June): 159-88.

Argues that Frost knew well the writings of James and that there are affinities between the two writers. Essay describes parallels and differences, focusing on the poetry of Frost.

28 SHEEHY, DONALD G. "Aphrodite and the Factory: Commercialism and the Artist in Frost and Cather." *South Atlantic Review* 51 (May): 49-63.

Compares and contrasts Frost and Willa Cather on the subject of commercial success and its effect on the artist.

29 ____. "The Poet as Neurotic: The Official Biography of Robert Frost." *American Literature* 58 (October): 393-410.

In examining Lawrance Thompson's biographical study some "essential problems of biography" are described. Argues that Thompson read and was influenced by Karen Horney's *Neurosis and Human Growth* as he "developed a psychological paradigm" for his task.

30 ____. "Robert Frost: The Figure a Poet Makes." *DAI* 48, 02A, p. 392. Ph.D. dissertation, University of Virginia, 236 pp.

On Frost's "autobiographical impulse" to create his biography to match his image of the poet as ordinary man.

31 SPIVACK, KATHLEEN. "The Frost Farm in Derry, New Hampshire." *The Beds We Lie In*. Metuchen, N.J.: Scarecrow Press, pp. 83-86.

Poem in seventeen quatrains.

32 STILLER, WALTER N. "The Dominion of Violence in the Poetry of Robert Frost." *Mid-Hudson Language Studies* 9, no. 1:65-73.

Describes the varieties of violence in Frost's poetry. Sees Frost as "the eternal wry humorist of human contradiction and chaos, [who] turns to the spectacle of human emotion with an inquisitive, fascinated eye."

33 ____. "The Measure of Meaning: The Concept of Order in the Poetry of Robert Frost." *DAI* 47, 10A, p. 1327. Ph.D. dissertation, City University of New York, 290 pp.

Sees Frost's sense of order as arising from a need for self-preservation against destructive Nature.

34 STORCH, MARGARET. "Robert Frost's 'The Subverted Flower.'" *American Imago* 43 (Winter): 295-305.

Examines the poem in light of psychoanalytical theories. Suggests that the central concept of the poem lies "in Frost's rejection of his mother's emotional hold over him and his reassessment of the values and roles handed on to him by his family."

35 SULLIVAN, D. BRADLEY. "'Education by Poetry' in Robert Frost's Masques." *Papers on Language and Literature* 22 (Summer): 312-21.

Finds that the masques "offer a powerful statement of Frost's open-ended approach to life, reminding us that all our structures of knowledge can only be 'momentary stays against confusion,' that language can never fully define or describe the experiences and meanings that it signifies."

1987

1 ABEL, DARREL. "Frost's 'In the Home Stretch.'" *Explicator* 45 (Winter): 37-39.

Describes the "thematic tensions that provide dynamics for most of Frost's poetry."

2 BUGEJA, MICHAEL J. "Mind and Essence in the Personification of Robert Frost." *Texas Review* 8 (Spring-Summer): 98-106.

Sees two kinds of personification in Frost's poetry. "One relates to state of mind; the other, to essence." Concludes that "mind and essence generate tension in his work, allowing Frost to impose his will on nature and to utilize the full range of personification, from abstraction to apostrophe."

3 CHALLENDER, CRAIG. "Robert Frost's Strategies of Syntax in Selected Letters, 'The Silken Tent,' and 'The Gift Outright.'" *South Carolina Review* 19 (Summer): 19-28.

Discusses how Frost's "syntax and punctuation (or lack of it) . . . reveal a knack for gritty detail, an impetuosity, a concern for verbal sound and function."

1987

4 COULTHARD, A.R. "Frost's 'Mending Wall.'" *Explicator* 45 (Winter): 40-42.

On the two characters in the poem. It "*is* an ironic self-revelation of character," exposing "Frost's cold mind posing as a warm heart." See also 1989.5.

5 EVANS, WILLIAM R. "Robert Frost: The Unpublished *Cardinal* Letter." *American Literature* 59 (March): 116-18.

Describes and prints the original version of a 1925 letter Frost wrote to Wilbert Snow of the board of editors of the *Cardinal* (Wesleyan University) concerning Edward Thomas. The letter had been changed when it was published.

6 FLEISSNER, ROBERT F. "Enveloped in That *Old Cloak*: Edward Thomas, Wordsworth, and Frost's Untaken Road." *South Carolina Review* 19 (Summer): 39-45.

Attempts to show the connecting influences of Wordsworth on Frost through Edward Thomas on "The Road Not Taken."

7 FRANCIS, LESLEY LEE. "Between Poets: Robert Frost and Harriet Monroe." *South Carolina Review* (Summer): 2-15.

Describes Frost's relationship with Monroe and her *Poetry: A Magazine of Verse*. Includes three photographs.

8 GOZZI, RAYMOND D. "Lowell's 'The Cathedral' and Frost's 'Happiness Makes Up in Height What It Lacks in Length.'" *Explicator* 45 (Spring): 28-30.

Suggests an influence of the early part of James Russell Lowell's poem on Frost's choice of a title for his poem.

9 JERSILD, DEVON, ed. "Frost Verbatim." *New England Review and Bread Loaf Quarterly* 10 (Autumn): 8-20.

Prints excerpts from the personal notes of Reginald Cook, retyped and compiled in three volumes that he called *Frost Verbatim* and presented to Middlebury College.

10 KEARNS, KATHERINE. "'The Place Is the Asylum': Women and Nature in Robert Frost's Poetry." *American Literature* 59 (May): 190-210.

Suggests that the "two figures, the disturbed woman and the love-crossed and naked madman, may be seen as emblematic, for Frost's poetry subtly but persistently reiterates a vision of sexual anarchy."

11 KJØRVEN, JOHANNES. *Robert Frost's Emergent Design: The Truth of the Self in-between Belief and Unbelief*. Oslo: Forlag A/S; Atlantic Highlands, N.J.: Humanities Press International, 203 pp.

Discusses religious skepticism in Frost's poetry; sees in the pulls of belief and unbelief "a search for answers to certain questions about self-identity."

12 MARCUS, MORDECAI. "Dickinson and Frost: Walking Out on One's Grief." *Dickinson Studies*, no. 63, pp. 16-29.

Compares Dickinson's "After a Great Pain a Formal Feeling Comes" and Frost's "Acquainted with the Night" as "great lyrics of loneliness, suffering and implied defense against it."

13 MONTEIRO, GEORGE. "Frost's Hired Hand." *College Literature* 14 (Spring): 128-35.

On the New England code of the hired man and possible parallels in popular journals.

14 ____. "Robert Frost in Brazil: An Interview." *South Carolina Review* 19 (Summer): 16-18.

Provides a translation of an interview in Rio de Janeiro in *Jornal de Comercio*, August 1954. Frost's advice to artists: "I would want them all to adhere to a single word from the Old Testament, from the Book of Hosea: 'similitude.'" See also 1988.24.

15 MOORE, RICHARD. "Of Form, Closed and Open: With Glances at Frost and Williams." *Iowa Review* 17 (Fall): 86-103.

Compares and contrasts the metrical forms of Frost and William Carlos Williams, "enlivening each other with their complementary energies: a precise and intricate formality that has the wonderful naturalness of one of Frost's great lyrics, and a careless freedom that somehow manages to be as memorable, as compelling."

16 NAPOLI, DONNA JO. "A Correspondence in Frost's Poetry and Its Significance for Metrical Theory." *Language and Style* 20 (Fall): 371-83.

Applies four linguistic theories to the metrics of several lines from the poems as Frost was recorded reading them.

17 NITCHIE, GEORGE W. Review of *Robert Frost Himself*, by Stanley Burnshaw. *New England Quarterly* 60 (June): 290-95.

See 1986.9. Describes the biography as "an angry attempt to discredit Lawrance Thompson's . . . biography." Finds the attempt unsuccessful, because of "overkill," humorlessness, and personal bias.

18 PATTERSON, ANNABEL. "Hard Pastoral: Frost, Wordsworth, and Modernist Poetics." *Criticism* 29 (Winter): 67-87.

Discusses Frost's political poem, "Build Soil," as a pastoral poem in the Romantic tradition represented by William Wordsworth.

19 PRITCHARD, WILLIAM H. "West of Boston: Robert Frost." *Yale Review* 76 (Spring): 380-85.

Recalls episodes with Frost at Amherst through many years.

20 RAGLE, THOMAS B. "A Reading of Robert Frost's 'The Mountain.'" In *Amerikanische Lyrik: Perspektiven und Interpretationen*. Edited by Rudolf Haas. Berlin: Schmidt, pp. 208-22.

Sees the poem as Frost's early statement of the relation of the pastoral-georgic poet to nature. It is "about man's relationship to Nature, to its otherness, to its elemental, ultimately mysterious forces which make it also and paradoxically the source of life and enlightenment."

21 ROTELLA, GUY. "Comparing Conceptions: Frost and Eddington, Heisenberg, and Bohr." *American Literature* 59 (May): 167-89.

On Frost's understanding of modern science, especially as revealed in his essay, "Education by Poetry." His knowledge of physics was current and modern.

22 SIMONS, JOHN. "Mise en Abysme and Tradition in Two New England Poems." *Journal of American Studies* 21 (April): 104-8.

Discusses "that old heraldic term designating the device whereby the image of a shield is represented on the surface of a shield," or, in literary terms, "to designate the way in which the operations of reading and writing are represented in the text, and *in advance*, as it were, of any other possible reading." Discusses the notion in "Mending Wall" and Robert Lowell's "Father's Bedroom."

23 STOUT, JANIS P. "Re-Visions of Job: *J.B.* and 'A Masque of Reason.'" *Essays in Literature* (Macomb, Ill.) 14 (Fall): 225-39.

Compares and contrasts Frost's and Archibald MacLeish's treatment poetically of the Book of Job.

24 STRANDBERG, VICTOR. "The Frost-Melville Connection." *Dutch Quarterly Review of Anglo-American Studies* 17, no. 3:171-81.

Sees affinities in the two writers in both theme and technique.

25 WALLACE, PATRICIA B. "Robert Frost and the Poetry of Survival." *South Carolina Review* 19 (Summer): 29-38.

Discusses Frost's poetry as deriving from self-preservation in the face of overwhelming personal tragedies.

1988

1 ABEL, DARREL. "'Against and With' in Robert Frost's Poetry." *Colby Library Quarterly* 24 (December): 205-11.

Finds the influence of "two of his acknowledged philosophical mentors, William James and Henri Bergson" in Frost's "Mending Wall."

2 ____. "Frost's 'Provide, Provide.'" *Explicator* 46 (Spring): 24-26.

Analyzes the poem in terms of its biblical allusions, especially the irony of the "witch" Abishag.

3 BENOIT, RAYMOND. "An American Hierophany: The Wood-Pile in Hawthorne and Frost." *Arizona Quarterly* 44 (Summer): 22-27.

Compares Frost's woodpile and Hawthorne's in *The Blithedale Romance*. Sees each as "a kind of Americanized Stonehenge – a Woodhenge – which 'shows, makes manifest, as Mircea Eliade wrote of hierophany, the coexistence of contradictory essences: sacred and profane, spirit and matter, eternal and non-eternal.'"

4 BIEGANOWSKI, RONALD. "Robert Frost's *A Boy's Will* and Henri Bergson's *Creative Evolution*." *South Carolina Review* 21 (Fall): 9-16.

Discusses Bergson's influence even in Frost's early work.

5 CARTER, EVERETT. "Frost's 'Design.'" *Explicator* 47 (Fall): 23-26.

Does not see the poem as "an expression of bitter cosmic irony . . . that finds the Universe either malignant or absurd." Suggests instead that the "principal tone is mockery" of various points of view about God and evil in the universe.

6 COULTHARD, A.R. "Robert Frost's 'The Road Not Taken.'" *Notes on Contemporary Literature* 18 (September): 11-12.

Sees the poem as poorly constructed. It is "a broken-back poem."

7 CRONENWETT, PHILIP N. "Frost Drafts Inscribed in Presentation Volumes." *Dartmouth College Library Bulletin* 28 (April): 75-81.

Bibliographical description of drafts of poems in copies of *Mountain Interval* received through Friends of the Dartmouth Library.

1988

8 CUSIC, DONALD F. "The Poet as Performer." *DAI* 49, 06A, p. 1455. Ph.D. dissertation, Middle Tennessee State University, 139 pp.

Discusses Vachel Lindsay, Frost, and T.S. Eliot. Sees Frost as "a consummate performer."

9 DORESKI, WILLIAM. "Robert Frost's 'The Census-Taker' and the Problem of Wilderness." *Twentieth Century Literature* 34 (Spring): 30-39.

Suggests that the speaker "does not dwell on religious matters but on humanist concerns, on the difficulty of maintaining a toehold of civilization in an abject waste."

10 FAGGEN, ROBERT. "Robert Frost and the Challenge of Darwin." *DAI* 49, 10A, p. 3026. Ph.D. dissertation, Harvard University, 356 pp.

On the influence of the Darwinian revolution on Frost's poetic mythology resulting in "a highly dramatic poetry, at once passionate and skeptical, of labor, domestication, and struggle."

11 FLEISSNER, ROBERT F. "Frost as Ironist: 'After Apple-Picking' and the Preautumnal Fall." *South Carolina Review* 21 (Fall): 50-57.

On the apple as biblical symbol and other religious connotations in the images of the poem.

12 ____. "New Lines by Robert Frost: His 'Addendum' to 'Mending Wall.'" *English Language Notes* 25 (March): 63-66.

Prints lines discovered on a holograph postcard in the Boston Public Library:

Some may know what they seek in school and church / And why they seek it there. For what I search / I must go meas'ring stone wall perch on perch.

Revised: 1989.7.

13 ____. "'The Phantom Wooer' and the Haunting Resonance: An Anticipation of Frost – or of Beddoes' Own Name?" *Names* 36 (March-June): 91-94.

Suggests that the words "Our bed is lovely" resemble "Beddoes Lovell," especially when a "Tomb-Tom" parallel is considered.

14 FRATTALI, STEVEN VINCENT. "Across the Field: Nature and Selfhood in the Poetry of Robert Frost." *DAI* 50, 05A, p. 1305. Ph.D. dissertation, State University of New York, Binghamton, 237 pp.

Discusses the poetry as influenced by Geoffrey Hartman, Emerson, and William James. Sees four major aspects of experience: "physical work, epistemological uncertainty, the preparation of the self for death, and a sense of ultimate estrangement from the natural world."

15 HOLLAND, NORMAN N. *The Brain of Robert Frost: A Cognitive Approach to Literature*. New York: Routledge, Chapman, and Hall, 200 pp.

"This is not a book about Robert Frost. . . . This is, I believe, the first book to bring to bear on literary criticism and theory the revolutionary discoveries of cognitive science and recent research into the brain." Includes rewritten versions of 1973.12, 1975.16, and 1984.16.

16 JANZEN, J. GERALD. "Reassessing Frost's Fair Impression and His Mistrust." *Religion and Literature* 20 (Autumn): 71-87.

Examines the word *mistrust* in Frost's usage, conceptually and dialectically, in the poems and the masques.

17 JOST, WALTER. "The Lurking Frost: Poetic and Rhetoric in 'Two Tramps in Mud Time.'" *American Literature* 60 (May): 226-40.

Discusses the tensions of contemplation-action and abstraction-practicality in the poem.

18 KATZ, SANDRA L. *Elinor Frost: A Poet's Wife*. Westfield, Mass.: Institute for Massachusetts Studies (Westfield State College), 193 pp.

Reprint of dissertation: 1983.19. Portrays sympathetically Frost's wife, Elinor White, beginning with high school courtship in Lawrence, Mass. Attempts to correct Thompson's view of "an unhappy and stern woman." Shows the influence of her attitudes and opinions on the poetry.

19 KERN, ROBERT. "Frost and Modernism." *American Literature* 60 (March): 1-16.

Suggests that Frost's ideas, if not the forms, were the same as those of the Modernists. Describes Frost's response to the "modern" poets–Pound, Hulme, Eliot–and his determination to be "new" in old ways.

20 KISTER, DANIEL A. "The Use of Nature in Kim Sowol and Robert Frost." *Korea Journal* 28 (February): 4-14.

Compares the work of a Korean poet of the twenties and thirties to that of Frost.

1988

21 LITTLE, GERALDINE C. "Birches: Peterborough, New Hampshire." In *A Well-Tuned Harp*. Upper Montclair, N.J.: Saturday Press, p. 33.

Twenty-four line poem in tribute to Frost as birch trees evoke his presence.

22 LLOYD-KIMBREL, ELIZABETH D. "A Condition of Complete Simplicity: Poetic Returns and Frost's 'Directive.'" *Worcester Review* 10 (January): 32-41.

Suggests that the area of Quabbin Reservoir near Amherst could be the locale of "Directive." Also makes comparisons of the poem with T.S. Eliot's "Little Gidding."

23 McCOY, JOAN D. "Frost's 'The Armful.'" *Explicator* 47 (Fall): 21-23.

On how Frost solves the problem "of maintaining in a disordered age the sense of order and unity that balanced and constructive living requires."

24 MONTEIRO, GEORGE. "The Brazilian Academy's Tribute to Frost." *South Carolina Review* 21 (Fall): 3-4.

Reprints remarks by Manuel Bandeira, perhaps Brazil's greatest poet, in the *Jornal de Comercio*, following Frost's visit in 1954. See also 1987.14.

25 ____. *Robert Frost and the New England Renaissance*. Lexington: University of Kentucky Press, 176 pp.

Describes the effects of earlier New Englanders – primarily Emily Dickinson, Thoreau, Emerson – on Frost's poetry. Also deals with Longfellow, William James, and others.

26 MORRISSEY, L.J. "'Mending Wall': The Structure of Gossip." *English Language Notes* 25 (March): 58-63.

"Despite the apparent message of 'brotherhood,' the poem's achievement is clear. Frost has structured a poem in which the message of brotherhood is enacted from the rhetorical stance of gossip, which excludes, isolates and distorts."

27 PARINI, JAY. "Robert Frost." In *Columbia Literary History of the United States*. Edited by Emory Elliott, et al. New York: Columbia University Press, pp. 937-46.

Sees Frost as "a complex, even difficult, poet of extraordinary power and lasting importance." The question of whether Frost is a "major" poet has been settled positively and permanently.

28 PERRINE, LAURENCE. "Frost's 'The Fear': Unfinished Sentences, Unanswered Questions." *College Literature* 15 (Spring): 199-207.

Reprint of 1984.29.

29 PETERS, JOAN D. "Education by Poetry: Robert Frost's Departure from the Modern Critical Tradition." *South Carolina Review* 21 (Fall): 27-37.

Argues that the critic must acknowledge Frost's belief that poetry is derived from "the close metaphorical relationship of art to life," in contrast with contemporaries who disavow educational goals.

30 STRANDBERG, VICTOR. "The Frost-Melville Connection." *Costerus: American Literature in Belgium*, n.s. 66:17-25.

Reprint of 1987.24.

31 STRONG, PAUL. "Robert Frost's 'Nighthawks'/Edward Hopper's 'Desert Places.'" *Colby Library Quarterly* 24 (March): 27-35.

Finds "striking" similarities in the lives and works of the two artists in both theme and method.

32 THOMAS, RON. "Thoreau, William James, and Frost's 'The Quest of the Purple-Fringed.'" *American Literature* 60 (October): 433-50.

On the choice of the purple orchis as symbol for Thoreau and Frost, James's "cognitive figure," and Frost's expression of his poetic identity in 1901 and his belief in eventual vindication as a poet.

33 THOMPSON, LESLIE M. "Robert Frost's 'Home Burial': The Ways of Death in American Society." *RE: Artes Liberales* 14 (Spring-Fall): 1-9.

Discusses the poem as it "reflects, through the use of the central framing device of the window, the far-reaching changes in attitude toward death, burial, and grief that occurred in America during the nineteenth and early twentieth centuries."

34 WALSH, JOHN EVANGELIST. *Into My Own: The English Years of Robert Frost, 1912-1915*. New York: Grove Press, 286 pp.

Provides a biographical portrait of Frost in the years before and during publication of his first two books. Describes relations with friends and acquaintances, preparation for a poetic career, sources for some poems, and early reviews.

1989

1 BROMWICH, DAVID. "The Sense of Vocation in Frost and Stevens." In *A Choice of Inheritance: Self and Community from Edmund Burke to Robert Frost*. Cambridge, Mass.: Harvard University Press, pp. 218-231.

Discusses "Two Tramps in Mud Time," comparing it with Stevens' "The Course of a Particular," both in terms of Wordsworth and "the egotistical sublime." Also contains a chapter entitled "Edward Thomas and Modernism," pp. 197-217.

2 CERVO, NATHAN. "Frost's 'The Road Not Taken.'" *Explicator* 47 (Winter): 42-43.

Compares Frost's "roads" to Rimbaud's "ruts," as in his *Illuminations*; sees both uses as "visionary."

3 CLARK, JOHN R. "Left on Right Track with Robert Frost." *Notes on Contemporary Literature* 19 (January): 10-12.

Replies to 1988.6. Disagrees that it is a "broken-back poem." Argues that the themes are "(A) ambivalence about stimuli and responses, causes and effects, and (B) contradictions in the course of time about the signification of experience."

4 COOK, REGINALD L. "Robert Frost." In *Sixteen Modern American Authors, Volume 2: A Survey of Research and Criticism since 1972*. Supplement by John McWilliams. Edited by Jackson R. Bryer. Durham, N.C.: Duke University Press, pp. 360-403.

Provides a bibliographical survey, in prose, of Frost criticism, with such headings as "Themes," "Sources and Influences," "Frost's Modernity." Supplement describes Pritchard's biography (1984.33) as what will be "the standard one-volume study of Frost, man and poet, for a good many years."

5 COULTHARD, A.R. "Three Wrong Turns on Frost's 'The Road Not Taken.'" *Notes on Contemporary Literature* 19 (May): 11-12.

Replies to 1989.3, 1989.8, and 1989.18, in defense of his prior article (1988.6).

6 FLEISSNER, ROBERT F. "From Stein to Frost: The Germinal Soil of a Rose Family" and "'*Sub Rosa*': Focussing on Frost's Flower as 'Five-Petaled.'" In *A Rose by Another Name: A Survey of Literary Flora from Shakespeare to Eco*. Locust Hill Literary Studies, no. 5. West Cornwall, Conn.: Locust Hill Press, 217 pp.

Examines rose imagery in literature through the ages to contemporary fiction in Umberto Eco's *The Name of the Rose*. Discusses nuances in Frost's use of the rose as metaphor and as symbol.

7 ____. "Robert Frost Stonewalls It Again: The Newly Discovered Variant Lines." *English Language Notes* 27 (December): 57-61.

Revision of 1988.12. Includes previously dropped information on "A Star in a Stone-Boat."

8 HOGGARD, JAMES. "Correcting an Error: 'The Road Not Taken.'" *Notes on Contemporary Literature* 19 (January): 7-8.

Replies to 1988.6. Sees the poem as speculative rather than reflective.

9 LENTRICCHIA, FRANK. "Lyric in the Culture of Capitalism." *American Literary History* 1 (Spring): 63-88.

Describes the poetic careers of Frost and Ezra Pound at their beginnings in 1913 and their subsequent divergences. Discusses "The Road Not Taken" as Frost's statement of choosing "a self and therefore an entire course of life." Consequently, the two poets have had "two different and mutually hostile readerships."

10 LEO, JOHN R., comp. "Frost, Robert." In *Guide to American Poetry Explication.* Vol. 2, *Modern and Contemporary*. Boston: G.K. Hall, pp. 157-91.

Provides a list, alphabetically by poem-title, of explications in articles and books since 1925.

11 MACK, ANNE, and J.J. ROME. "Marxism, Romanticism, and Postmodernism: An American Case History." *South Atlantic Quarterly* 88 (Summer): 605-32.

Describes types of critical perspectives, using "Stopping By Woods . . . " to illustrate some kinds of critical approaches. Sees the influence of Dante Gabriel Rossetti on the poem.

12 MONTEIRO, GEORGE. "The Facts on Frost." *South Carolina Review* 22 (Fall): 87-96.

On Frost's verification of factual details in the poems.

13 MORRISSEY, CHARLES T. "Who Persuaded Robert Frost to Matriculate at Dartmouth? The Case of the Mysterious Alumnus." *Dartmouth College Library Bulletin* 29 (April): 46-58.

Suggests, "with cautious certitude," that the man was John Crockett Sanborn, Jr., a Dartmouth graduate and a teacher at Lawrence (Mass.) High School when Frost was a senior there.

14 OSTER, JUDITH. "The Figure a Marriage Makes." *South Carolina Review* 22 (Fall): 109-19.

On Frost's poems about marriage.

15 PERKINS, DAVID. "Robert Frost and Romantic Irony." *South Carolina Review* 22 (Fall): 33-37.

Using "Design," Frost is shown as an ironist like the English Romantic poets.

16 PRITCHARD, WILLIAM H. Introduction to *Poems by Robert Frost: "A Boy's Will" and "North of Boston."* New American Library. New York: Signet, 160 pp.

Presents Frost's first two books in their original form, including poems not published since the first edition. Comments on Frost's technique of modulating voice in the poems.

17 ROOD, KAREN L. "Robert Frost." In *Dictionary of Literary Biography: Modern American Poets: James Dickey, Robert Frost, and Marianne Moore*. Documentary Series: An Illustrated Chronicle, vol. 7. Edited by Matthew Bruccoli, et al. Detroit: Gale Research, pp. 127-252.

Provides a general overview of highlights of Frost's life and career, with extensive facsimile reproductions of manuscripts and letters, as well as photographs of Frost, his family, friends, and residences. Includes significant reviews of Frost's books, and a bibliography.

18 SCRIMGEOUR, J.D. "Another Path: An Alternative Reading of 'The Road Not Taken.'" *Notes on Contemporary Literature* 19 (January): 8-10.

Replies to 1988.6. Sees the poem as "explosive and terrifying."

19 SIMIC, CHARLES. "Visionaries and Anti-Visionaries." *Denver Quarterly* 24 (Summer): 114-23.

Discusses Frost, Wallace Stevens, and Emily Dickinson as Emersonian "visionary skeptics."

20 VAN EGMOND, PETER, and GOU XI-QUAN. "Robert Frost." In *The Major American Poets: An Introduction*. Shanghai, People's

Republic of China: Shanghai Foreign Languages Education Press, pp. 175-203, 449-468.

Prints "The Pasture," "Mending Wall," "The Death of the Hired Man," "After Apple-Picking," "The Road Not Taken," "Birches," "Nothing Gold Can Stay," "The Runaway," "Stopping by Woods on a Snowy Evening," and "The Silken Tent." In English in Part 1 of the book and Mandarin in Part 2, with explanatory notes throughout.

21 WELTMAN, SHARON ARONOFSKY. "The Least of It: Metaphor, Metamorphosis, and Synecdoche in Frost's 'The Subverted Flower.'" *South Carolina Review* 22 (Fall): 71-78.

Describes the emotional changes in the couple in the poem.

22 WILCOX, EARL J. *Robert Frost: The Man and the Poet*. 2d ed. Lanham, Md.: University Press of America, 176 pp.

Reissue of 1981.53.

1990

1 ABEL, DARREL. "Frost's 'Fragmentary Blue.'" *Explicator* 48 (Summer): 270-72.

On Frost's use of the color blue as "names of conditions or . . . states of things" and not as mere description.

2 ALLPORT, SUSAN. "Stone Symbols of Shaker Permanence." *New York Times*, 13 May, Section 20, p. 9.

Article in Travel Section on the Shaker Village in Canterbury, N.H. Photo identified as Frost's farm there, although Frost is not mentioned in the article.

3 BAILIS, MOIRA. "Robert Frost." Letter to the Editor. *New York Times*, 24 June, Section 20, p. 34.

Corrects 13 May identification of photograph as Frost's farm in Derry, N.H., where he lived in 1900-1909, not at Shaker Village in Canterbury.

4 BUCCLEUGH, STEPHEN H. "Robert Frost's 'The Road Not Taken.'" *Notes on Contemporary Literature* 20 (November): 3-4.

Discusses the final two lines of the poem and concludes that the speaker "knows that the naiveté of youth will be replaced by the rationalization of old age."

1990

5 CALHOUN, RICHARD J. "The Figure a Poet Makes." *South Carolina Review* 23 (Fall): 191-92.

Review of 1985.25 and 1989.22. Finds Wakefield's book "unattractive in format but serviceable in its content," its main argument sound. Discusses some recent reprints of critical books on Frost.

6 DOXEY, WILLIAM. "'The Road Not Taken' as Modernist Search for Meaning in a Meaningless World." *Notes on Contemporary Literature* 20 (September): 12.

Suggests that "the persona's (or Frost's) awareness that regardless the road that he should've or might've taken, he's stuck with the one he took, so he might as well view it favorably."

7 EVANS, WILLIAM R. "Robert Frost and Helen Thomas: Five Revealing Letters (Part 2)." *Dartmouth College Library Bulletin* n.s. 30 (April): 38-44.

Describes the reason for Frost's break with the wife of friend Edward Thomas: her books about life with her husband and their love affair were too sexually explicit and made the Frosts angry and unhappy with her. After 1928, Frost avoided her and refused to reply to her letters.

8 FLEISSNER, ROBERT F. "Avoiding Detours: Frost's 'The Road Not Taken.'" *Notes on Contemporary Literature* 20 (September): 7-8.

Reiterates the assertion that Wordsworth's "Lucy" influences Frost's meaning in the poem.

9 GRAY, RICHARD. "Traditionalism, Scepticism, and Tragedy: Frost." *American Poetry of the Twentieth Century*. Longman Literature in English Series. New York: Longman, pp. 131-38.

Sees Frost as "the supreme example of the sceptic in modern American poetry: the person who mistrusts categorical answers, utopian solutions, and who, for reasons he thoroughly articulates, cannot or will not make up his mind."

10 HOELLER, HILDEGARD. "Evolution and Metaphor in Robert Frost's Poetry." *South Carolina Review* 23 (Fall): 127-35.

Describes Frost's reading of Darwin and his reaction as more "against the idea of an all-encompassing scientific theory and against Darwinism than against the idea of evolution itself." Discusses "Accidentally on Purpose," "West-Running Brook," and "The White-Tailed Hornet" in this light.

11 INGEBRETSEN, EDWARD J. "Unlettered (Robert Frost's Farm, Franconia, New Hampshire)." *South Carolina Review* 23 (Fall): 83.

Twenty-four-line poem.

12 KATZ, SANDRA. "'The World is Evil': Personal Experience Dramatized in 'Home Burial.'" *South Carolina Review* 23 (Fall): 122-26.

Does not see the poem as merely autobiographical: "The personal experience is the death of Frost's son, but the female and male characters are not simply Elinor and himself. At times, Elinor's voice is heard in the male's voice, Frost in the female's. In addition, other voices are blended into the characters."

13 LENTRICCHIA, FRANK. "The Resentments of Robert Frost." *American Literature* 62 (June): 176-200.

Examines the publishing history of influential American poetry anthologies in the twentieth century, especially those of Louis Untermeyer. Frost's reaction was "an antinomian intention to undo all design (all intention, all structure) in its institutional incarnation and sanction."

14 MILLER, LEWIS H., Jr. "Frost's Old Man and Hawthorne's Judge Pyncheon: An Intertextual Reading." *Papers on Language and Literature* (Summer): 358-69.

Sees parallels in "An Old Man's Winter Night" and Hawthorne's depiction of old age, death, and disorder in *The House of Seven Gables*.

15 POIRIER, RICHARD. *Robert Frost: The Work of Knowing*. Stanford: Stanford University Press, 330 pp.

Reissue of 1977.30.

16 POSTEMA, JAMES ALLEN. "Time and Timelessness in Robert Frost's Lyrics." *DAI* 50, 11A, p. 3592. Ph.D. dissertation, University of Illinois, Urbana-Champaign, 290 pp.

Traces "temporal conflicts that arise between timeless, narrated moments in Frost's lyrics and the temporarily anchored moments from which speakers narrate the poems. Such conflicts highlight contradictions at the heart of the lyric form – both in Frost's work and in all lyrics."

17 SHEEHY, DONALD G. "(Re)Figuring Love: Robert Frost in Crisis, 1938-1942." *New England Quarterly* (June): 179-231.

Describes Frost's courtship and marriage to Elinor White and his subsequent love for Kathleen Morrison and their effect on his essay, "The Figure a Poem Makes," in which "Frost confirmed at a time of deepest crisis what throughout he had put on record for the discerning: The career of the poet could be in itself a figure for love."

18 SOKOL, B.J. "Bergson, Instinct, and Frost's 'The White-Tailed Hornet.'" *American Literature* 62 (March): 44-55.

Sees the poem as Frost's reaction to Bergson's *Creative Evolution* as one of "complex and ramified doubt." Uses Frost's own annotated copy of Bergson as source.

19 WALLERSTEIN, NICHOLAS PERRY. "Poetic Quarrel: The Rhetoric of Antithesis in Modern Poetry." *DAI* 50, 9A, p. 2894. Ph.D. dissertation, University of Oregon, 244 pp.

"This dissertation traces, analyzes, and evaluates a particular form of antithesis used for structural, rhetorical, thematic, and ideological effect in which an adversative conjunction ('but' or 'yet') is used to introduce toward the end of a poem an antithetical statement." Uses "But I have promises to keep" as one example.

Addendum

1970

1 ADAMS, RICHARD P. "Permutations of American Romanticism." *Studies in Romanticism* 9 (Fall): 249-68.

Sees American romanticism as moving to a view of the universe as dynamic, not static, and seeking a means to control it. Emerson, Frost, and Stevens are, therefore, "romantic."

2 ALLISON, EILEEN. "Robert Frost's Poetic Treatment of Human Relationships." *DAI* 31, 08A, pp. 4148-49. Ph.D. dissertation, University of Notre Dame, 180 pp.

Deals with two categories of human relationships: poems that are about intimate human relationships and those about less intimate relationships (neighbors, strangers, employers-employees).

3 BRAVERMAN, ALBERT, and BERNARD EINBOND. "Frost's 'Two Tramps in Mud Time.'" *Explicator* 29 (November): Item 25.

Describes the emotional complexity of seasonal imagery in the poem.

4 D'AVANZO, MARIO L. "Frost's 'A Young Birch': A Thing of Beauty." *Concerning Poetry* 3 (Fall): 69-70.

Suggests lines from Keats's "Endymion" (I, 12-14) as a possible source.

5 DUFFY, MARTHA. "A Poet Revealed." *Time* 96 (31 August): 70-71.

1970

Review of Thompson, *Years of Triumph*. "Calling this record of human fragility and failure *Years of Triumph* is either a heavy-handed attempt at irony or reflects the kind of complacency that Frost at his worst could achieve. Thompson is reasonably fair to Frost the man, but more compassion would have yielded a larger, more reflective picture of the poet."

6 EPSTEIN, JOSEPH. "A Mean, Miserable Man–But as a Poet One of the Best." *Book World (Washington Post)* 13 September, pp. 3, 6.

Review of Thompson, *Years of Triumph* (1969). Suggests that Thompson is "unprotective," because he is "unstintingly honest," thus managing "to nail Frost to the barn door."

7 HARNETT, RUTH. "Two Poems by Robert Frost." *CRUX: A Journal on the Teaching of English* (Pretoria, South Africa) 4 (February): 20-28.

Discusses "Mending Wall" and "Stopping by Woods. . . ." Sees the poems as simple, yet complex, and Frost as equivocal, adding depth of tone and texture.

8 HOLLAND, NORMAN N. "The 'Unconscious' of Literature: The Psychoanalytic Approach." *Contemporary Criticism*. Stratford-Upon-Avon Studies, 12. London: Edward Arnold, pp. 130-53.

Analyzes "Mending Wall" in a psychoanalytic approach and finds evidence of "oral fantasy" of gratification, as in infancy. Reprinted: 1988.15.

9 JACOBSKIND, BARBARA RACHEL. "Nature Images in the Poetry of Robert Frost: A Three-Part Study (Concordance, Dictionary, Analysis)." *DAI*, 31, 12A, p. 6554. Ph.D. dissertation, Brown University, 428 pp.

Attempts to provide a clear explanation of Frost's nature images for "a world of ever-increasing urbanization, wasting resources, and threatening extinction of natural species of plant and animal life," images which future readers eventually may find unfamiliar and confusing.

10 VENDLER, HELEN. "A Disastrous Life." *New York Times Book Review*, 9 August, pp. 1, 34-35.

Review of Thompson's *Years of Triumph* (1969). Sees a presentation of Frost's life as a disaster, "a monster of egotism, a self-protective man leaving behind him a wake of destroyed human lives."

11 VINSON, ROBERT S. "The Roads of Robert Frost." *Connecticut Review* 3 (Fall): 102-7.

Examines the road as symbol in the poetry, using three headings: "Leaving the Road," "Return to the Road," and "The Road Out." Specifically determines roads as different from paths and highways that have other significances.

1971

1 ARTZT, NORBERT. "The Poetry Lesson." *College English* 32 (April): 740-42.

Imagines discussing "Dust of Snow" in class with an intelligent but recalcitrant female student.

*2 BARRY, ELAINE. "Robert Frost as a Literary Critic." AACO23677. Ph.D. dissertation, Rutgers-The State University of New Jersey.

Revised for publication: 1973.2.

3 BORROFF, MARIE. "Robert Frost's New Testament: Language and the Poem." *Modern Philology* 69 (August): 36-56.

Explores Frost's stylistic simplicity in *A Boy's Will*, *North of Boston*, and *Mountain Interval*, and "how these bear on broader questions of dramatic strategy and structure." Reprinted in 1979.9.

4 COMBELLACK, C.R.B. "Frost's 'Spring Pools.'" *Explicator* 30 (November): Item 27.

Rebuts David Toor (*Explicator* 28 [November 1969]: Item 28), and suggests that the water image is not confusing.

5 GEYER, C.W. "A Poulterer's Pleasure: Robert Frost as Prose Humorist." *Studies in Short Fiction* 8 (Fall): 589-99.

Discusses Frost's early prose pieces on chicken farming.

6 GIERASCH, WALTER. "Frost's 'The Silken Tent.'" *Explicator* 30 (September): Item 10.

Examines some implications of the imagery in the poem, especially silk.

7 MASTENDINO, ALFRED CHARLES. "Dualism in the Poetry of Robert Frost." *DAI* 32, 04A, p. 2095. Ph.D. dissertation, University of Massachusetts, 413 pp.

Examines "the underlying structure of Gnostic dualism contained in the major poetry of Robert Frost."

1971

8 PERRINE, LAURENCE. "Frost's 'Dust of Snow.'" *Explicator* 29 (March): Item 61.

"The way in which a crow shakes down dust of snow on Frost's speaker is left unspecified, thus permitting several possibilities. I see them chiefly as four: beautifully, animatedly, cheerily, and humorously."

9 ____. "Frost's 'Gathering Leaves.'" *CEA Critic 34* (November): 29.

Uses the word *crop* to describe three possible interpretations of the poem.

10 ____. "Frost's 'The Mountain': Concerning Poetry." *Concerning Poetry* 4 (Spring): 5-11.

Offers a "fanciful" reading of the poem: that it is a poem about poetic and scientific truth.

11 SHACKFORD, JOHN STEVEN. "The Development of the Poetry of Robert Frost." *DAI* 32, 05A, p. 2708. Ph.D. dissertation, Indiana University, 203 pp.

Examines three characteristic modes of Frost's poetry: a psychological character study, based on a dream or dream-like story; a symbolic mode, based on maintaining a tension between a literal and a symbolic level of meaning; and an ironic bardic mode, based on treating a serious theme in a style that is humorous and seemingly casual or even whimsical.

12 STANFORD, DONALD E. "Thompson's Frost and Bailey's Hardy." *Southern Review* 7 (Autumn): xvii-xxi.

Sees Thompson's biography as disturbing in its apparent vindictiveness. Compares the scholarship to J.O. Bailey's *The Poetry of Thomas Hardy: A Handbook and Commentary*, which Stanford finds superior.

13 TOLIVER, HAROLD E. "Frost's Enclosures and Clearings." In *Pastoral: Forms and Attitudes*. Berkeley: University of California Press, pp. 334-60.

Examines the metaphors of the road, the boundary line and clearing, the woods, the spring pools, and the streams and the "ways in which they convert the landscape of New England into the symbolic materials of poetry."

14 VAIL, DENNIS. "Frost's 'Ghost House.'" *Explicator* 30 (October): Item 11.

Suggests that "the speaker is both present and absent, the time is both present and past, and the poem's real subject is memory."

*15 VOGT, VICTOR E. "Modes of the Dramatic in the Poetry of Robert Frost." AACO237024. Ph.D. dissertation, University of Chicago.

1972

1 ABAD, GEMINO H. "Stopping by Woods: The Hermeneutics of a Lyric Poem." *Diliman Review* (Quezon City, Philippines) 20 (January): 25-40.

Examines the poem as "a dramatic lyric" in which "the medium is not simply language as such but language as action."

2 ATKINS, BRUCE BENJAMIN. "Robert Frost: The Orthodoxy of the Self." *DAI*, 32, 11A, pp. 6411-12. Ph.D. dissertation, University of Wisconsin, 266 pp.

Attempts "to substantiate two related hypotheses: (1) While critics have acknowledged Frost's achievement in the lyric form and in the dramatic narrative ... they have overlooked Frost's use of a parable technique in much of his best poetry; (2) Frost's poetry declined in achievement as the poet grew older mainly because of the incursion into his verse of ideological opinion which caused him to violate his parable technique."

3 BASS, EBEN. "Frost's Poetry of Fear." *American Literature* 43 (January): 603-15.

On the various types of fear in Frost's poetry, particularly "inner" and "outer" sources of fear. Examines the theme in several poems.

4 BOYD, JOHN D. "Frost's Grafting in His 'Birches.'" *Descant* (Texas Christian University) 16 (Fall): 56-60.

Examines the two parts of the poem as described in Brooks and Warren, *Understanding Poetry*, third edition (1960). Discusses metonymy in "Birches" and other poems.

5 BUTLER, DAVID WARREN. "Robert Frost and the Clearing in the Wilderness." *DAI* 33, 07A, p. 3634. Ph.D. dissertation, University of Wisconsin, 217 pp.

Examines the "central image of the clearing in the wilderness ... to reveal the artistic coherence of [Frost's] work as a whole." Defends the poetry against charges that it lacks consistency, or "is whimsical, superficial, and irresponsible."

1972

6 COOK, MARJORIE ELIZABETH. "Robert Frost: The Challenge of Conflict." *DAI* 33, 02A, p. 748. Ph.D. dissertation, Southern Illinois University, 250 pp.

Discusses Frost's methods of dealing with human conflict with "what may seem to be compromised ideals: strategic retreat, straight crookedness, and those 'rough zones'–the limitations of man."

7 DILLINGHAM, RICHARD. "The Value of Social Conservatism According to Robert Frost." *South Atlantic Bulletin* 37 (November): 61-65.

Describes various manifestations of Frost's conservatism as revealed in the poetry.

8 FITZGERALD, GREGORY, and PAUL FERGUSON. "The Frost Tradition: A Conversation with William Meredith." *Southwest Review* 57 (Spring): 108-17.

Edited from a television tape made on 7 April 1971, in connection with the *Writers Forum* program at the State University of New York, Brockport. Meredith reads "In Memory of Robert Frost" from his *Earth Walk: New and Selected Poems* (1970) and comments on Frost's influence.

9 HANNUM, WILLIAM E., Jr. "The Religious Attitudes of Robert Frost." *DAI* 33, 03A, p. 1142. Ph.D. dissertation, University of Virginia, 140 pp.

Examines Frost's attitudes toward religion in terms of "institutional religion, welfarism, science and religion, the relationship between metaphysical and physical nature, and the violence in human nature."

10 HARRIS, EARLE GLENN. "Bond and Free: Robert Frost's Early Poetry, 1913-1923." *DAI* 33, 08A, pp. 4415. Ph.D. dissertation, Indiana University, 178 pp.

Sees in Frost's first four books a development from a self-conscious evasion to an emphasis on pastoral reflection, which "suggests that Frost is not irresponsible or anti-intellectual as some critics would claim."

11 HAYNES, DONALD T. "The Narrative Unity of *A Boy's Will*." PMLA 87 (May): 452-64.

Shows how Frost's first book traces "the development of a poet from initial withdrawal to final return to society, and from initial interest in, to final, mature acceptance of his poetic vocation."

12 KITTREDGE, SELWYN. "'Stopping by [the] Woods on a Snowy Evening'–Without Tugging at the Reins." *English Record* 23 (Fall): 37-39.

Comments on the lack of a possessive or a definite article for "woods," suggesting that the poem "rebukes man for his folly in attempting to reduce nature to the meanness of acquisitive values."

13 KOH, BYRON HYUN. "Robert Frost as Survivalist." *DAI* 33, 09A, p. 5183. Ph.D. dissertation, University of Massachusetts, 242 pp.

Deals with Frost's real and poetic strategies for handling "urgent concerns." Discusses images, metaphors, symbols, and attitudes to show a variety of strategies.

14 LAMBDIN, WILLIAM G. "Frost's 'The Oven Bird.'" *Explicator* 31 (September): Item 3.

Compares the singing in the poem to elements of jazz music.

15 LATHEM, EDWARD CONNERY, and LAWRANCE THOMPSON, eds. *Robert Frost: Poetry and Prose*. New York: Holt, Rinehart and Winston, 480 pp.

Prints selected poetry and prose, with many omissions. Focuses on materials external to the poetry, with numerous textual changes.

16 LORD, RUSSELL HINCKLEY, Jr. "A Study of Robert Frost's Theory of Sentence Tones and Some of its Early Modifications." *DAI* 33, 04A, p. 1734. Ph.D. dissertation, Boston University, 256 pp.

Provides biographical and artistic sources for Frost's idea of "sentence sounds," such as expressed in "The Figure a Poem Makes."

17 McQUADE, DONALD ANTHONY. "Convergences of Style: A Study of the Affinities between Robert Frost and Ralph Waldo Emerson." Part 2. *DAI* 32, 12A, p. 6936. Ph.D. dissertation, Rutgers-The State University of New Jersey, 195 pp.

Second part of a three-subject, not interrelated. Examines "stylistic affinities between Frost and Emerson by comparing their uses of language, voice, and points of view through a detailed reading of each writer's work."

18 MONTEIRO, GEORGE. "Frost's 'After Apple-Picking.'" *Explicator* 30 (March): Item 62.

"The poem can be seen as an elaboration of *Genesis*: Adam's curse was not merely that his doom was henceforth to live by the 'sweat' of his 'face,' but that the curse to labor would follow him into his rest and his dreams."

19 ____. "'Good Fences Make Good Neighbors': A Proverb and a Poem." *Revista de Etnografia* (Portugal) 16: 83-88.

Suggests several sources for the proverb as far back as the Middle Ages in Spain. The saying itself is a sort of wall in the poem, preventing communication.

20 MORRIS, JOHN. "The Poet as Philosopher: Robert Frost." *Michigan Quarterly Review* 11 (Spring): 127-34.

Discusses Frost's "Maple" and the biblical meaning of the "wave-offering." Sees the influence of Henri Bergson in other poems.

21 PERRINE, LAURENCE. "The Dilemma of Frost's 'Love and a Question.'" *Concerning Poetry* 5 (February): 5-8.

Suggests two interpretations: literal and semiallegorical.

22 ____. "Frost's 'An Empty Threat.'" *Explicator* 30 (April): Item 63.

In the poem "Frost whimsically expresses the temptation he sometimes feels to leave a world of simple moral choice and heroic action."

23 REED, KENNETH. "Longfellow's 'Sleep' and Frost's 'After Apple-Picking.'" *American Notes and Queries* 10 (May): 134-35.

Describes Frost's indebtedness to Longfellow.

24 RUESCH, LORA ANN. "Man and Nature in the Poetry of Robert Frost." *DAI* 33, 09A, p. 5196. Ph.D. dissertation, Purdue University, 187 pp.

Examines the subject of nature in Frost's poetry as written by one who "did not believe that a cognizant Being created the universe. . . . Frost's aim was to write poetry for an age in which man can no longer believe in God."

*25 SEARS, JOHN FRANKLIN. "Strongly Spent: Fate, Time, and Process in the Poetry and Poetics of Robert Frost." AACO31858. Ph.D. dissertation, Harvard University.

26 STILLIANS, BRUCE. "Frost's 'To the Thawing Wind.'" *Explicator* 31 (December): Item 31.

Suggests that Frost's poem is "a critique of poetic pretense in Shelley's 'Ode to the West Wind.'"

1972

27 TURPIN, ELIZABETH RICE. "Rhetoric and Rhythm in Twentieth-Century Sonnets by Hopkins, Auden, Frost, Cummings, Thomas, and Merrill Moore." *DAI* 33, 08A, p. 4368. Ph.D. dissertation, Texas A&M, 385 pp.

Deals with Frost as a sonneteer, but studies Hopkins and Merrill Moore in much greater detail.

28 TYLER, DOROTHY. Review of Thompson, *Years of Triumph*, 1969. *Michigan Quarterly Review* 11 (Spring): 135-36.

Straightforward review, finding some of Thompson's critics too harsh.

29 VAIL, DENNIS RAY. "Robert Frost's Imagery and the Poetic Consciousness." *DAI* 33, 07A, p. 3678. Ph.D. dissertation, Cornell University, 162 pp.

Deals with Frost as a realist and a symbolist. Examines Frost's imagery as within his "realistically and empirically based esthetic."

30 VAN DORE, WADE. "In Robert Frost's Rubbers." *Michigan Quarterly Review* 11 (Spring): 122-26.

Reproaches Frost's biographer, Lawrance Thompson, as "Frost-deficient." Suggests that he never stood in Frost's shoes, or rubbers, and that he should have "put them on and taken to farming instead of becoming a conventional professor writing a biography."

31 _____. "Robert Frost: A Memoir and a Remonstrance." *Journal of Modern Literature* 2 (November): 554-60.

Remonstrates against Lawrance Thompson for biographical inaccuracies. Concludes: "Frost was a rascal with rascals, but he was saintly when dealing with humble deserving individuals."

32 WATKINS, FLOYD C. "The Poetry of the Unsaid: Robert Frost's Narrative and Dramatic Poems." *Texas Quarterly* 15 (Winter): 85-98.

Describes the first nine years of Frost's career as his best because he "learned to leave much unsaid. He learned restraint, the limits of poetry. . . . Paradoxically, Frost's best poetry is a combination of fact and the unstated and unknown."

33 WEINSTEIN, NORMAN. "Robert Frost's Ideas of Order." *Language and Literature* 1, no. 1:5-21.

Begins with the notion that Frost is not modern. Attempts to describe Frost's "world" and the structure of his poems in terms of mathematics, examining "numerical relationships."

1973

1 BARNES, DANIEL R. "Frost's 'Putting in the Seed.'" *Explicator* 3 (April): Item 59.

On the sexual elements in the poem.

2 BARRY, ELAINE. *Robert Frost*. New York: Frederick Ungar, 145 pp.

Reprint of 1971.2. "Frost is not among the great poets, though he is among the very good ones." Examines the "voices" in the poems.

3 CLARK, DAVID R. "An Excursus upon the Criticism of Robert Frost's 'Directive.'" *Costerus*, o.s. 8:37-56.

Summarizes all previous commentary on the poem and concludes that "examination of it will not soon cease, and the question whether or not it makes an overt assertion of religious values will be debated again."

4 DANIEL, CHARLES LEE. "Imagery in the Poetry of Robert Frost." *DAI* 34, 04A, p. 1900. Ph.D. dissertation, Florida State University, 221 pp.

Studies Frost's images by categorizing into animate-inanimate, heat-cold, light-dark, and the "dark woods" and the "star" images.

5 DENDINGER, LLOYD N. "The Ghoul-Haunted Woodland of Robert Frost." *South Atlantic Bulletin* 38 (November): 87-94.

Discusses Frost's affinities with Edgar Allan Poe in "the applicability of Poe's theories to much of Frost's poetry; and the similarities in the allegorical use the two poets make of the natural world."

6 ____. "Robert Frost in Birmingham." *Ball State University Forum* 14 (Summer): 47-52.

Recounts a tape-recorded story told by Richebourg Gaillard McWilliams, visiting professor at the University of South Alabama, 1970-71, concerning a Frost visit and talk there, a very successful enterprise.

7 FLEISSNER, ROBERT F. "A Comment and Correspondence on Robert Frost: Frost's Use of Coleridge's Nocturnality." *Literary Criterion* (Bombay) 10 (Summer): 67-72.

Takes issue with an article in this journal (Winter 1969) by C.D. Naramsimhaiah, on Frost's reading of the English Romantic poets and their possible influence on such poems as "Acquainted With the Night."

8 _____. "Frost's 'Not All There.'" *Explicator* 31 (January): Item 33.

Suggests "the point of the poem is that the speaker did not find God there because he himself was only half there."

9 FOSTER, RICHARD. "Leaves Compared with Flowers: A Reading in Robert Frost's Poems." *New England Quarterly* 46 (September): 403-23.

Shows "how loss can make [Frost] turn from flowers and petals to the contemplation of leaf and bark, fern and lichen. 'Leaves Compared With Flowers' is a dark companion to 'Putting in the Seed.'"

10 GREINER, DONALD J. "The Use of Irony in Robert Frost." *South Atlantic Bulletin* 38 (May): 52-60.

Suggests that Frost's "suspicion of the three human comforts, God, communion with nature, and human companionship," leads him to turn his irony on those themes.

11 HALL, DOROTHY JUDD. "Robert Frost: Contours of Faith: A Study of a Poet's Religious Belief." *DAI* 34, 04A, p. 1911. Ph.D. dissertation, Boston University, 331 pp.

Reprinted as book in 1984.10. Traces the influence of both Old and New Testament thought, and of certain philosophers – namely Emerson, William James, and Henri Bergson – whose idea helped to buttress Frost's religious thinking." Concludes that Frost was "a man of deep religious conviction who regarded the writing of poetry as a spiritual vocation."

12 HOLLAND, NORMAN N. "A Touching of Literary and Psychiatric Education." *Seminars in Psychiatry* 5 (August): 287-99.

Offers a physician's analysis of "Once By the Pacific" to show how "literary experience should play a vital role in the original and continuing education of all psychiatrists to this way of recreating for themselves the human beings they treat." Reprinted: 1984.16.

13 HORST, BERNARD L. "Robert Frost: Problems of Persona." *DAI* 34, 08A, p. 5176. Ph.D. dissertation, Fordham University, 252 pp.

Frost created not one, but several personae: Walker, Farmer, Astronomer, Quester, Keeper, Poet, Fearer, and others, as a kind of cast of characters.

14 JAYNE, EDWARD. "Up against the 'Mending Wall': The Psychoanalysis of a Poem by Frost." *College English* 34 (April): 934-51.

1973

Sees "a doubly inverted theme of homosexual spring courtship denied" in the two characters in the poem. Finds the submerged theme in other English and American poets as well.

15 "John F. Kennedy: Poetry and Power." *Washington Post*, 22 November, Section A, p. 18.

Recalls, on the tenth anniversary of Kennedy's assassination, the events of his inauguration and Frost's participation as poet in it.

16 KIRK, RUSSELL. "Robert Frost: No Ideologue." *National Review* 25 (23 November): 1302.

"It is interesting to speculate on what great national blunders might have been averted, had Robert Frost been appointed President Kennedy's privy counselor, rather than merely the performing poet at the Kennedy inauguration."

17 LENTRICCHIA, FRANK. "Robert Frost: The Aesthetics of Voice and the Theory of Poetry." *Criticism* 15 (Winter): 28-42.

Examines Frost's poetry in terms of the theories of Clive Bell and Walter J. Ong.

18 LINDNER, CARL M. "Robert Frost: Dark Romantic." *Arizona Quarterly* 29 (Autumn): 235-45.

Compares Frost to another "dark romantic": Herman Melville.

19 LYCETTE, RONALD L. "The Vortex Points of Robert Frost." *Ball State University Forum* 14 (Summer): 54-59.

"Vortex points . . . are highly subjective symbols and metaphors of form that arise from our encounters with commonplace rituals, objects, and concepts. They are temporary and transient, like a ring of smoke, like the seasons, and like time itself; they are also generally subjective – until objectified and structured by the artist."

20 "The Mertins Collection of Robert Frost." *Bancroftiana* (Berkeley), no. 55 (June): 11-12.

Briefly describes the circumstances surrounding the Frost collection presented to the University of California Bancroft Library by Louis and Esther Mertins.

21 MONTEIRO, GEORGE. "Robert Frost's Linked Analogies." *New England Quarterly* 46 (September): 463-68.

Compares the themes of "Mending Wall" and "The Tuft of Flowers" to raise "interesting possibilities."

22 MOORE, ANDY JOHNSON. "Topical Philosophy of Robert Frost: Science, Politics, Social Philosophy, Education." *DAI* 34, 05A, p. 2643. Ph.D. dissertation, University of Texas, 200 pp.

Examines Frost's attitudes and opinions concerning each of the four fields. Sees influence of Emerson and Thoreau.

23 PERRINE, LAURENCE. "'Two Tramps in Mud Time' and the Critics." *American Literature* 44 (January): 671-76.

Finds the speaker of the poem being a good neighbor, as Frost would be, in giving the wood-chopping job to the strangers "for pay."

24 "Robert Frost: A Poem for a President." *Washington Post*, 22 November, Section A, p. 18.

Reprints "Preliminary History in Rhyme," which was to be read at the inauguration of John F. Kennedy, but because of the glare of the sun, "The Gift Outright" was recited instead.

25 STANLIS, PETER J. "Robert Frost: The Individual and Society." *Intercollegiate Review* (Bryn Mawr) 8, no. 5:211-234.

Examines Frost's belief that "there was a natural identity of self-interest and social benevolence in both individuals and society which kept men together or in society," although adjustments were always necessary.

26 UTLEY, FRANCIS L. "Robert Frost's Virgilian Monster." *English Language Notes* 10 (March): 221-23.

Corrects Lawrance Thompson's (*Years of Triumph*) "misreading" of "The Self-Seeker." Sees the *Aeneid* as a source for Frost's "Monstr'."

27 VAIL, DENNIS. "Tree Imagery in Frost's 'Mending Wall.'" *Notes on Contemporary Literature* 3 (January): 9-11.

Suggests that the characters in the poem are typified by the differences between apple trees ("unaggressive" with "a potential for happiness") and pine trees ("somber and humorless").

28 VANDER VEN, TOM. "Robert Frost's Dramatic Principle of 'Oversound.'" *American Literature* 45 (May): 238-51.

Discusses two comments by Frost on poetry: statements about a theory of poetry and his belief that good writing must be dramatic. "The unit of writing he most frequently discussed he called variously the 'sentence-sound,' 'sound-posturing,' and the 'sound of sense.' This unit he regarded as the primary dramatic element in poetry."

1973

29 WILBUR, RICHARD. "Poetry's Debt to Poetry." *Hudson Review* 26 (Summer): 273-94.

Discusses several poets on the notion that "art begets art." Sees a parallel between "Stopping by Woods . . ." and Thomas Lovell Beddoes' "The Phantom-Wooer."

Index of Authors

Note: Entries dated prior to 1974 are located in the Addendum

Index of Titles

Note: Entries dated prior to 1974 are located in the Addendum